Liturgy of Life

Liturgy of Life

donald hilton

An anthology compiled by
Donald Hilton based on
patterns of Christian Worship

NCEC

Other books by Donald Hilton

Boy into Man
Girl into Woman
Celebrating Series
Six Men and a Pulpit
Risks of Faith
Raw Materials of Faith
Results of Faith
After Much Discussion

Compiled by Donald Hilton

A Word in Season
Prayers for the Church Community
(with Roy Chapman)

Cover design:
Mike Ayers

Published by:
National Christian Education Council
Robert Denholm House
Nutfield
Redhill, RH1 4HW

British Library Cataloguing-in-Publication Data:
Hilton, Donald, *1932 –*
    Liturgy of life
    1. Christianity : public worship
    I. Title
    264

ISBN 0-7197-0760-9

First published 1991
Collection © Donald Hilton 1991

Typeset by One and A Half Graphics, Redhill
Printed by BPCC-AUP Aberdeen Ltd.

Contents

To my sister,
Margaret
9 February 1991

*Love is not changed by death and nothing is lost
and all in the end is harvest*

Edith Sitwell

lit-ur-gy (littarji) n., pl. -gies.

A system of public worship in the Christian Church. [Late Latin *liturgia* from Greek *leitourgia*, public service, service of a priest, from *leitourgos*, public servant, minister, priest: *leos* (stem *leit*), variant of *laos*, people, multitude + *ergon*, work]

Liturgy, the work of the people

Preface

The patterns of worship followed by the mainstream churches are very similar to each other. The same elements of worship can be seen in them all. The order in which they are followed varies only a little.

Confession and a recognition of God's forgiveness come early in most acts of worship, God is praised, and thanks are given for his many gifts. By either sermon or creed the faith is affirmed. Jesus Christ is celebrated and honoured. Prayers are offered for a peace which includes personal wholeness, creative human relationships, and the care of the vulnerable and deprived.

In the Roman Mass, the Free Church service, the Salvation Army Meeting, and the Orthodox Liturgy the same elements can be identified.

But none of the attitudes we express in worship are exclusive to the sanctuary. They are everyday attitudes expressing common experiences. It is not only in churches that we say 'thank you' and 'sorry'; we do that in families and supermarkets. Praise is given in schools and offices as well as in worship. In all manner of relationships we 'carry burdens' for others, and at deeper levels of friendships we share burdens of sorrow, or even guilt. Thus, however uncertainly, we walk where Christ trod and glimpse the meaning of the cross. Liturgy is more that a pattern of worship; liturgy is the everyday work of the people.

This anthology follows the structure of the Mass. My own experience of the Mass has been more in the concert hall than the sanctuary. Amongst others, Palestrina and Mozart, Gounod and Giles Swayne have been my priests. I value their ministry. Within that structure *Liturgy of Life* portrays those everyday, outside-the-sanctuary experiences and thoughts which interlock with the main elements of Christian worship. It is intended both to aid personal devotion and also to provide material for Christian education and worship.

Donald Hilton   Leeds
                                                                                          1991

Lord, have mercy

> *Lord, have mercy,*
> *Christ have mercy,*
> *Lord, have mercy.*

Lord have mercy

The apostle Paul pinpoints the problem: 'the good which I want to do I fail to do; but what I do is the wrong which is against my will'. The parable of the scorpion (*item 7*) simply expresses the truth in story form, as do the opening chapters of Genesis. Morris West makes Franz Lieberman say in 'The Tower of Babel', 'Each one of us is a battleground between good and evil' (*item 9*).

The effect of sin is monstrous. Let loose, it destroys relationships (*item 23*), creates wars (*item 19*), abuses the vulnerable (*items 12-14*)) closes hospitals (*item 18*), and turns the Sabbath into a weapon (*item 24*). We worship death (*item 20*).

The life of Christ must run its complete and self-sacrificing course before we begin to see an answer. Because we long for a better way but know our helplessness, we can only fall on our knees and beg: 'Lord, have mercy on us!'

1   Have mercy
    Upon us.
    Have mercy
    Upon the efforts,
    That we
    Before Thee,
    In love and in faith
    Righteousness and humility,
    May follow Thee,
    With self-denial, steadfastness and courage,
    And meet Thee
    In the silence.

    Give us
    A pure heart
    That we may know Thee,
    A humble heart
    That we may hear Thee,
    A heart of love
    That we may serve Thee
    A heart of faith
    That we may live Thee,

    Thou
    Whom I do not know
    But Whose I am

    Thou
    Whom I do not comprehend
    But Who has dedicated me
    To my fate.
    Thou –

    Dag Hammarskjöld, from *Markings*

2 Because he loved him dearly, God one day revealed to Moses the place where the great treasures are stored which will, at the end of time, be given as rewards to the pious and the just. He explained each treasure, and who would receive it, in great detail.

One gift was reserved for those who, in their earthly life, had given alms to the poor; another for those who had supported widows and orphans. A further gift was reserved for those who had given generously to support the worship of the temple. For those who had faithfully kept the Law yet another precious treasure was in store. In this way He continued to show to Moses the gifts of heaven, and who would receive them.

At length He came to one treasure of enormous size and value. 'For whom is this treasure reserved?' Moses asked, God answered: 'Out of the treasures I have already shown you, I give rewards to those who have deserved them by their deeds; but out of this treasure I give to the undeserving, for I am gracious to those who are not deserving, generous to those who can lay no claim to my generosity, and bountiful to those who do not deserve my bounty.'

A Jewish parable.

3 People often think of Christian morality as a kind of bargain in which God says, 'if you keep a lot of rules I'll reward you, and if you don't I'll do the other thing.' I do not think that is the best way of looking at it. I would much rather say that every time you make a choice you are turning the central part of you, the part of you that chooses, into something a little different from what it was before. And taking your life as a whole, with all your innumerable choices, all your life you are slowly turning this central thing into either a heavenly creature or into a hellish creature.

C.S. Lewis, from *Mere Christianity*

4   When God first tried his prentice hand
    At making worlds like grains of sand,
    And creatures of the strangest kind
    Had finally evolved a mind,
    Ate from the tree of good and ill,
    And learned to procreate and kill,
    Did he then, seeing what had come
    From his design, beneath the sun,
    Feel something new, which had no name
        Till Adam christened it as shame?

W.S. Beattie

5   A fire burns within my heart
    consuming hope, strength and trust
    Deep in my mind is a spark
    of torment, frustration and fear.
    Who can lift the yoke
    of toil and turmoil?
    Who can lift the curse
    imposed on me from birth
    and heal the wound
    which never bleeds?
    Who can break the chains
    that bind me
    to sin, misery and crime?

    'Have I become a thing amongst things?
    A beast among creatures
    and a tool among weapons?
    I waited,
    perhaps too long
    to hear the wind whisper
    'brother, you are free'.
    The freedom to listen to justice
    or a baby cry
    or a leaf falling from a tree.

Colin Bowes

6 The Making of the World

On the first day God made light,
And he was dazzled and made dark,
And then a switch.

On the second day God made the earth
And he took the elements,
Shuffled them,
And dealt them.

On the third day God made plants.
He learnt to breathe the fresh air
Before it was too late,
And he saw beauty.

On the fourth day God made the stars
And God was proud of them.
He winked at them
And they winked back.

On the fifth day God made birds and fish
And wanted conversation,
But they would not talk.

On the sixth morn he made animals to talk to
But they wouldn't listen,
And in the evening he made man.
He said, 'Man, my companion',
And man said, 'Off my land,
You're trespassing.'

On the seventh day God rested
And thought.
And he never saw the eighth day.

Nick Midgley, 13 years

7 Prisoner to the law of sin (*Romans 7.24*)

A scorpion came to the bank of a river and could not cross because the river was in flood. Happily, the scorpion saw a fish, contentedly nibbling the weeds in the shallows of the river. 'Please, fish' said the scorpion, 'let me climb onto your back, and carry me across the river'.

The fish was quick to reply. 'Never,' he said, 'for if I carry you on my back, you will sting me and I shall die.'

But the scorpion had a ready and persuasive answer. 'Not so. If I sting you and you die in the middle of the river, I too will die because I cannot swim. I shall surely drown'.

The fish was reassured, took the scorpion onto his back, and began to swim across the flooded river. Half way over, the scorpion gripped the fish, and stung him. With his dying breath, the fish asked plaintively, 'Why did you do it? Now we shall both die.'

Replied the scorpion, 'I wish I knew, little friend. I wish I knew. It's just the way I am.'

8 Until the day he dies

'How do you compromise,' demanded Baratz harshly, 'when you're looking down the barrel of a gun?'

'Unfortunately,' said Franz Lieberman softly, 'we never compromise until we realize that the man who presses the trigger and the man he kills are the same person.'

'I don't understand that.'

'Let me try to explain. I think – all my experience confirms me in the belief – that the root of dissension is the struggle of the individual to discover, affirm and maintain his personal identity against all that threatens or appears to threaten it . . . The struggle begins at the moment of birth. The tiny human animal is set adrift in a strange and hostile ambience. He is no longer comfortable in the warm fluid of the womb. His nourishment is no longer automatic. He is subject to heat and cold, to hunger and pain, to the eccentric attentions of other human beings, whom he knows only by touch and smell, by the fact that they bring him comfort or discomfort. From that first tragic moment he finds that his desires and demands are thwarted, that he is forced, on the one hand, to accommodate himself and, on the other, to assert himself with his feeble resources, against those who are stronger than he. Even before he knows, before he knows that he knows, he is in conflict. He has begun his dialectic with life, an argument that will last until the day he dies.'

Morris West, from *The Tower of Babel*

9 'What is it, Franz . . . what is it that pushes us always to the point where our own life seems to depend on the death of another man, where our own trees will not grow unless we ravage the garden of the man next door?'

'The old man seemed to absorb the question like a sponge soaking up water. He dilated with it painfully as if he were bursting with thoughts he could not express. The light shone like an aureole on his white hair and made dark shadows and high bright peaks on his troubled face. He did not speak for a long while. It was as if he were obsessed with visions, filled up with prophesy for which he was denied an utterance. At last he answered, slowly and uncertainly:

'I ask myself the same question every day. I lie awake wrestling with it. Many of my patients are sick because of the terror of it. There has to be an answer, else all man's life and all man's effort is reduced to a nonsense.'

'That's the frightening thing,' said Yehudith. 'The absurdity of it all. You think you've made a sensible pattern, then it turns into an obscene jumble.'

Franz Lieberman gave her a swift, shrewd look.

'Why do you call it obscene?'

'Because that's what it is. One moment you see the human image clean and strong like a Greek statue – the next moment it's defaced and twisted out of all recognition. Walk two hundred metres from my garden and you'll step on a mine and be blown to pulp. But people put the mine there. People like us. We say we're builders, lovers, creators – but we're destroyers too, a pin prick under our skins. I get my name from a woman who made a man drunk and cut off his head.'

There was so much self-mockery in her tone that Baratz was shocked; but the old man sat quietly weighing the bitter words and his own gentle answer.

'I know what you mean ... Nobody has ever yet explained evil out of the world. I have patients who are literally mad with malice. It has become the focus of their whole lives, so that there is no room for the simplest decency to another human being. They make me believe in the old Biblical stories of diabolic possession – Saul striking at David with his spear in a repeated madness of jealousy and hate . . . But there is good too, child. I have a little nurse from Algeria who walks these same people in the garden and soothes them with her talk and her touch, as David soothed Saul with his music. Even though sometimes they have had to be restrained from hurting her, she still comes back smiling to try again.'

'You make me feel ashamed.'

'No . . . there's no shame. Each one of us is a battleground between good and evil.'

Morris West, from *The Tower of Babel*

10 If there was a God

Noah strokes the animals and they crowd around him.
And then there is another thing . . . but mind this is just between ourselves – between friends, eh?

He looks about to be sure they are alone, then speaks very quietly.
God isn't with us any more . . . Sh! . . . There!

The animals lower their heads brokenly.

Well, put yourselves in His place. Try to put yourselves respectfully in His place. Everyday, all day long, hearing His existence doubted, even at times when it is most apparent. It was all mankind before, now it's these children. Always asking Him for proofs and miracles; demanding – ah, it's too much – guarantees! 'If you are God, give us something else for dinner.' 'If you are God, take away my toothache.' 'If there was a God, He wouldn't have let me bang my head coming upstairs this morning.' Yes, my friends, that was what one of the little girls dared to say today. So He's gone off on a holiday, you see. Well, you can't really blame Him, all I can say is it's a wonder He didn't do it long ago. Goodness knows He's had patience enough. Well, He hasn't any more, that's all. After all, He's not a saint, that man. Just think of it, my friends, God! Almighty God! (The TIGER howls.) Now, now, never mind. He'll come back. He's gone to have a little rest, that's all.

He's just shut up shop for two or three weeks. All right, we'll wait 'till He opens up again.

. . . *The other animals howl with the TIGER.*

Andre Obey, from *Noah*

11 Once in a holy passion
I cried with heartfelt grief,
'Lord, I am vile and wicked -
Of sinners I am chief!'

Then stooped my guardian angel
and whispered from behind,
'Vanity, my little man!
You're nothing of the kind!'

From *The Ponteland Church Review*

12 Does that mean I'm dumb?

I think it's dumb to be a slow learner.
I don't like to be me.
It feels awful to be handicapped.
Some of us have problems.
Lots of us have no friends.
Some kids call us rejects.
I feel dumb to be behind.
Some kids throw books and erasers at me

Bob Jansen

13   So what if I'm awkward
always wiggling and shaking.
    So what if I'm clumsy,
always dropping and breaking.

    So what if you have trouble
understanding what I'm trying to say.
    Does that mean I'm dumb?
NO WAY

Heidi Janz, 14 years

14 I've had to seek out
Further safe passages,
Turn away when mindless children
Stare and whisper.
Mentally it hurts
Though they do not understand,
They think life's one easy road,
No bumps, no potholes, no troubles at all.
These pressures are like mountains,
Never ending.
But you have to keep going
Staring life right in the face,
Overcoming every obstacle
Risking everything.

Richard Field

15   In the slum

In the slums
Jewel staring eyes
    Of human flies
    Crowd the rims
    Of our social order.

We avoid
The stench of slums
Everything uncomfortable
Insistence
Of staring eyes
Evidence
Of substanceless limbs.

Here are –
Bilious houses
At the womb-head
Of comfort.
Riches
Pleasure.

Here are –
Magnificent skeletons
With shrinking skins
Shrinking
With our approval
Here
Here is
The world we accept
From our glass houses.

George Campbell

16   In Paradise with me

This day I will be with you in Paradise.
Paradise Place, Lord? I know it well.
Back to back houses with back to back people.
Not like the old days:-
Streets ringing with laughter like washing
And neighbours popping in like pints.
Now scullery rats run scared and scream
And television winks in jest
Like some surrogate company.
People bolt all contact out.
Old age lies battered on the kitchen floor,
And young unemployed sit in solo empty rooms.
Families feud, boarding up their turmoil from prying eyes,
And hope awaits its demolition.
A reconstruction job in Paradise Street, Lord.
Will you meet me there?

John Rawnsley

17   Father, Forgive

The hatred which divides nation from nation, race from race, class from class
FATHER, FORGIVE
The covetous desires of people and nations to possess what is not their own.
FATHER, FORGIVE
The greed which exploits the work of human hands and lays waste the earth.
FATHER FORGIVE.
Our envy of the welfare and happiness of others.
FATHER, FORGIVE
Our indifference to the plight of the imprisoned, the homeless, the refugee.
FATHER, FORGIVE.
The lust which dishonours the bodies of men, women and children.
FATHER FORGIVE.
The pride which leads to trust in ourselves and not in God,
FATHER, FORGIVE

Be kind to one another, tenderhearted, forgiving one another, as God in Christ forgave you.

Coventry Cathedral Prayer

18 Requiem for a hospital

When they found a body in the ditch
(in times past) they would take it into Church
And the priest would sing a Requiem,
For the murdered man to rest in peace
And that there might be forgiveness,
Lest outrage destroy that community.

Today our hospital lies murdered,
For they have torn out its heart
And I, the priest, will sing my Requiem
So that we, the cheated, may rest in peace
And that we may be able to forgive,
Lest the fire of our outrage burns us up.

I will sing my Requiem for those
Who have been misled by lies,
Half-truths and being kept in the dark.
I sing for the tears of old ladies
Fearing the future and of leaving
A day-room which had become their home.

I will sing my Requiem whilst beholding
White-faced fury in decent, respectable
Middle-aged women whose dear parent
Becomes a package to be shipped elsewhere.
From thinking that people can be juggled
Like papers on a desk: Good Lord, deliver us!

I will sing my Requiem for nurses
Whose years of patient, kindly caring
Counts for nothing when money is short.
I sing also for caterers, cleaners and porters.
From the idolatry of Mammon and
The illusion of Accounts: Good Lord, deliver us!

I will sing my Requiem for a Town
Whose past prudence and present charity
Has been hijacked 'for the good of everyone'
(So they say) without even an apology.
May it please Thee to forgive them
And to turn their hearts. And from hatred,
Malice and all uncharitableness:
Good Lord, deliver us!

Roy Akerman
Written when a hospital was closed against the wishes of many

19 **Afterwards?**

Afterwards it wasn't quite so bad
as might have been expected –
the holocaust also destroyed
every scrap of memory, produced
a sort of universal amnesia
and a human race (so far as they
remained human) with no trace
no recollection of the past,
neither history nor any impression
of that last incredible combustion
before the impossible present where
their strange half-life continued
amidst the cold, the stench, the dust.
Only, much later, a chance discovery
of some old records – papers, microfilm –
described the green world of before the blast
somewhere called Eden, which they labelled
primitive myth of a poetic mind.

Kenneth Wadsworth

20 We worship death in our quest to
possess ever more things;
we worship death in our hankering after
our own security,
our own survival, our own peace,
as if life were divisible
as if love were divisible
as if Christ has not died for all of us.

To you we lift our outspread hands and
thirst for you in a thirsty land.

From *A Litany of Penitence* in the Vancouver Worship Book

21 Mill-stones round the neck

We settled down again at school and I was moved up into the Big Room, as it was called. It was getting on into the autumn when I got another job. The Sister at the Hospital wanted a Yard Boy to carry coal for the wards and asked the School Mistress to find a suitable one. I was picked on, and went meat for manners*. I crept about very carefully not to drop coal or make a noise in the wards, pleasing the Sister-in-Charge, and was nearly too good to live, having become very religious.

My school teacher had told us of heaven up above, the starry heights far above the blue sky, where all good girls and boys went to live for ever with God and his angels. That heaven was beyond space, and the stars were windows which God looked through to see what bad boys and girls were doing down below. If they quarrelled or took that which didn't belong to them they would be thrown into a great pit, where there was fire and brimstone burning for ever.

I thought, small as I was, I won't last long – should soon be burnt up in a fire like that – having burnt myself a time or two with Mother's fire. Give me a terror of such a place and asked where it was. Teacher told us it was the home of the devil, and he use a long fork to stir the fire now and again and poke back the ones who try to get out. The boy sitting next to me say, 'Why don't he burn too?' But I told him, 'Hold yer row - or both of us'll git the cane.'

George Baldry, from *The Rabbit Skin Cap*

* 'meat for manners' – 'work for keep'

22 Double-standards

When we think of the history we learned in our childhood it must strike many of us that the morality taught through that history was often very strange. In your religious teaching, in your ethical education, you learned that to steal, to rob, and to lie were great crimes, and if you killed someone you would be put in prison and perhaps lose your own life. But if you lied, cheated, and killed for the advantage of your country it was a noble thing, and you were considered a great patriot and a great man. This double moral standard must be abolished if a real betterment of the world is to be achieved, and in this direction the religious teachers of the people have a great mission indeed.

Fritjof Nansen

23 I enjoyed the Dame school. It was owned and run by a Miss Tapp.
To assist her she had a staff of four mistresses and a matron. A man
came in to take us for soccer and cricket. I particularly liked being
a Wolf Cub and adored what the Wolf Cub book described as trekking.
I found the work in form fairly easy, though I got rather stuck in
arithmetic (all forms of mathematics were always an almost organic
weakness with me). I was only once acutely unhappy. The two senior
boys in charge allowed us all to go into the school field. Miss Tapp
objected to this and reprimanded them. They said I had told them
she had given permission. I hadn't. But Miss Tapp said she trusted
the two senior boys and knew that they couldn't both be lying, so
I must be. The three of them went on at me so much that in the end
I confessed to the lie, though I hadn't told it. I was given an order-
mark, and when the order-mark book was read out on Saturday
morning, Miss Tapp commented on mine and said it was for lying,
a particularly nasty offence. We were standing in a line and I hung
my head in shame, perfectly innocent though I was. It seems to me
now that there must have been something wrong between me and
my parents for my not telling them anything about it. Perhaps I
thought that, if I did, I should be given too big a dose of Jesus. I
don't know. In any case the incident wasn't at all typical. The school
was extremely well run and I enjoyed it.

H.R. Williams, from *Some day I'll find you*

24 'Thank Heaven!' said Clennam, when the hour struck, and the bell stopped.

But its sound had revived a long train of miserable Sundays, and the procession would not stop with the bell, but continued to march on. 'Heaven forgive me,' said he, 'and those who trained me. How I have hated this day!'

There was the dreary Sunday of his childhood, when he sat with his hands before him, scared out of his senses by a horrible tract which commenced business with the poor child by asking him in its title, why he was going to Perdition? - a piece of curiosity that he really, in a frock and drawers, was not in a condition to satisfy - and which, for the further attraction of his infant mind, had a parenthesis in every other line with some such hiccupping reference as 2 Ep. Thess. c iii, v.6 & 7. There was the sleepy Sunday of his boyhood, when, like a military deserter, he was marched to chapel by a picquet of teachers three times a day, morally handcuffed to another boy; and when he would willingly have bartered two meals of indigestible sermon for another ounce or two of inferior mutton at his scanty dinner in the flesh. There was the interminable Sunday of his nonage; when his mother, stern of face and unrelenting of heart, would sit all day behind a bible - bound, like her own construction of it, in the hardest, barest, and straightest boards, with one dinted ornament on the cover like the drag of a chain, and a wrathful sprinkling of red upon the edges of the leaves - as if it, of all books! were a fortification against sweetness of temper, natural affection, and gentle intercourse. There was the resentful Sunday of a little later, when he sat down glowering and glooming through the tardy length of the day, with a sullen sense of injury in his heart, and no more real knowledge of the beneficent history of the New Testament than if he had been bred among idolaters. There was a legion of Sundays, all days of unserviceable bitterness and mortification, slowly passing before him.

Charles Dickens, from *Little Dorritt*

25 I had this job, see
in the Bantu Labour Offices.
Those people, slow's the word,
and all busy dodging the rules.
Anyone'd think the Homelands
were pestilent. Only interested
in raking in the highest wages.
And the women – dead set on the city.

Well, I died. Shock, that.
No time even to draw my pension
(which was the main reason I joined).
At the gate Peter stood;
didn't wave me on, like I was expecting.
After all, haven't I done my best,
been a good husband, worked for the kids,
kept my home going?
He read out from his book,
I tell you I didn't like his tone:
'You have separated
wives from their husbands,
torn homes apart, taken men's work away from them,
sent exiles to a far country.'
Me! I ask you!
'All I did, Sir,
was to carry out orders
as decently as possible.'

But he'd gone, leaving me this form –
Permit to stay in area refused.
ENDORSED OUT.

I'm taking it up
with a higher authority.

Jill King

26 Repentance

Repentance is not striving to bring one's conduct into line with the Law or with the higher righteousness demanded by Jesus. Neither is it a painful scrutiny of one's motives with a view to substituting, let us say, unselfish for selfish motives. It is a return of the whole personality to God, a submission of the will to his will, the acceptance of his authority . . . The change itself is made possible by the new experience of God as Jesus reveals him, that is, as the merciful loving Father who seeks and saves the lost.

T.W. Manson

27 . . . both Adams met in me

We thinke that Paradise and Calvarie,
Christ's Crosse, and Adam's tree, stood in one place;
Looke, Lord, and finde both Adams met in me;
As the first Adam's sweat surrounds my face,
May the last Adam's blood my soule embrace.

John Donne

28 . . . not only the men and women of goodwill

O Lord, remember not only the men and women of goodwill but also those of ill will, But do not only remember all the suffering they have inflicted upon us.

Remember the fruits we bought, thanks to the suffering: our comradeship, our loyalty, our humility, our courage, our generosity, the greatness of heart which has grown out of all this. And when they come to judgement, let all the fruits that we have borne be their forgiveness.

Prayer of a condemned Jew in Belson

Glory to God in the highest

Glory to God in the highest,
and peace to his people on earth.

Glory to God in the highest

As Meister Eckhart suggests (*item 36*), perhaps it is better to be silent before the glory of God. Every description we offer is hollow; every experience of his glory is no more than a passing shadow.

Yet his glory forbids silence. Reflecting God's glory, creation bids us shout and sing: 'Glorious the song, when God's the theme.' (*item 48*). And we ourselves share the experience: 'Within man's face is mirrored God.' (*item 46*).

29   Lord God
I meet you
in the mystery
of life
the sudden silences
intensity of presence
that makes me
stop
catch my breath
lift up head
high
to catch the glory
of your moment

and then
bow
low
lost in the misery of my meagre self

so small
so weak
so far

from you.

God
you are of a grandeur and glory
I long after
and shrink from.

Have mercy!
In your glory
let your pity

touch me.

Nicola Slee, *Kyrie Eleison*

30 The purpose of our life
is God's glory.
However lowly a life is,
that is what makes it great.

Oscar Romero

31 Praise God! The signs of his glory –
　　like smoke-signals
　　　　in still air
　　like distant drums
　　　　through the jungle
　　like satellite transmissions
　　　　across the world –
nudge us into new awareness.

　Lord, we lift our eyes and hearts
　to greet your coming triumph.

Praise God! The signs of his glory
　　turn desert hunger
　　　　into daily satisfaction
　　turn less than enough
　　　　into more than enough
　　turn cul-de-sacs
　　　　into new openings –
and enlarge our experience.

　Lord, we lift our eyes and hearts
　to greet your coming triumph.

Praise God! The signs of his glory
　　reveal a goal
　　　　that lights up our starting-point
　　reveal a promise
　　　　that shapes our path
　　reveal the living Christ
　　　　who walks alongside us –
and wonderfully changes our lives.

　Lord, we lift our eyes and hearts
　to greet your coming triumph.

Kate Compston

32 Heart stopping
    breath holding
    cover my head,
    bare my feet.
    God is here.

    Heart stopping,
    breath holding
    sink to my knees.
    God is here.

    Heart stopping
    breath holding,
    He touches me
    warm fire explodes
    singingly
    inside my head.
    God is here.

    Heart stopping
    breath holding,
    I dare to look
    at the face of God.
    Oh joy –
    He
    knows
    me.

    Beth Webb

33 O God, O nameless Someone
That which contains all things yet is not contained,
Be there
What is this in me that cares, that prizes caring above
all material things,
But You?
What is this that feels there should be meaning?
Something through and beyond the pain and cruelty
Ravaging this world?
Is it You?
What is this that is so deeply personal?
That longs for that intimate closeness
That yet can be separate?
That seeks to create, to bring out of chaos
An order that is not confined?
That loves beauty and laughter
And that sheer zest of living?
Is it You?

And is it You in the darkness of our minds,
The injustice, the cruelty, the hurricane?
Can it be You in the evil?
Are You buried there?
You Who permeate the universe and beyond,
Gloriously transcendent and yet immediately immanent
Within the minutest particle?
O God, O Nameless Someone,
Be there.

Ceciley Saunders

34 God is not someone great and glorious
with power and majesty
he has no position, no first place
nowhere in this world.
No one becomes better because of God
he is no use to anyone, misery is still misery
he does not mend you when you are broken
he does not intervene in any dispute
(not even in the church)
he is not 'the answer to every question'
(as a popular religious teenage song
would like him to be)
he does not solve anything
there in Southeast Asia
between Washington and Hanoi.

You must love him
as he is:
not a God, not a spirit,
not a person, not an image,
Eckhart said
in the thirteenth century.

He is not the light of day
but darkness and emptiness
he is not a high tree of life
but a shapeless branch
he is not the immense sea
but a cup of water at the most
a spoonful of water to combat thirst.
He is not a mighty voice
but a vulnerable silence.
Lonely and despairing God,
like a man who is looking for another man
and cannot find him.

Huub Oosterhuis

35 impossible God, God with a name of nothing,
little God who cannot hold his own
against people,
against their gods of money and violence.
God of Jesus.

What will always happen to him
is what happened
to the powerless man from Nazareth.
He goes the way of every seed,
he is always the least of men.
All poverty is the poverty of God,
everything that is small and humiliated
reminds us of him.

Believing, praying is
enduring with the God of Jesus
or, according to Bonhoeffer,
sharing in the suffering of God
participating in the impotence of God
in this world.

Huub Oosterhuis

36 God has no name, for no one can say or understand anything about
him . . .
Thus if I say 'God is good', that is not true; I am good but God is
not good . . .
   And if I also say 'God is wise', that is not true. I am wiser than
he. If I say yet again, 'God is a being', that is not true; he is a being
above being . . . a master says, 'If I had a God whom I could know,
I would not regard him as God . . .'
   'You must love him as he is: neither God, nor spirit, nor image;
even more, the One without commingling, pure, luminous . . .'

Meister Eckhart (1260-1327)

37 If we could see God...

Of course
if we could see God,
we wouldn't be lolling lazy in pews
or thinking about the vicar's ears,
or whether our shoes hurt.
If – we could see God.

Of course we have faith!
We come to Church:
'happy are those who believe without seeing'...
(why *does* that woman let her boy
pick his nose?)

> ... Hush, listen to the wind sighing
> in the silence
> *... put your finger here and look at my hands*
> *... look at me*

We do not dare breath
with the joy and the wonder of it.
We are held in deep silence.
... Then comes a great shout.
We are become as translucent
as rainbows!
Stretching up to the very sky with joy.
– because we have seen the Lord!

Beth Webb

38 I know the spirit in this mortal frame
Marked with personality and name
Can, by awareness, any given hour
Ally itself with God. Then all the power
That floods the Universe with living light
Can surge and flow through me, and lift my sight
To higher levels, hushed and glad and free,
Until I know that God is touching me.
But like a child with book or game or ball
The span of my attention is so small!

Louise Sullivan

39 *In Peter Shaffer's play Amadeus, about the composer Mozart, Salieri, an older composer, tells of his relationship with God.*

Let me confess to you at once that as a boy in the lost little town of Legnago, I was the most ambitious fellow for a hundred miles around. I wanted – it was quite simple – everything my parents hated. I mean Fame. A fame that would precede me everywhere into the chambers of the Great! Not to deceive you, my dear confessors, I wanted to blaze like a comet across the firmament of Europe! And yet only in one especial way. Music. It alone has ever told me that there is any value in life. A note of music is either right or wrong, *absolutely. Questo o quello.* No middle course. Already when I was ten a spray of sounded notes could make me dizzy – quite literally – almost to falling down. By twelve I was stumbling about in the countryside, humming my arias and anthems to the Lord. My only desire was to join all the composers who had celebrated His glory through the long Italian past. Every Sunday I saw Him in church, staring down at me from the mouldering wall. Understand I don't mean Christ. The Christs of Lombardy are simpering sillies with lambkins on their sleeves. No. I mean an old candle-smoked God in a mulberry robe, staring at the world with dealers' eyes. Tradesmen had put Him up there. Those eyes made bargains – real and irreversible. 'You give me so – I'll give you so. No more: no less.'

'The night before I left Legnago forever, I went to see Him, and made a bargain with Him myself. I was a sober sixteen, filled with a desperate sense of right. I was to be taken next day to Venice by a family friend, and allowed to study music! Determinedly I screwed up my courage, and entered the church for the last time. I knelt before the God of Bargains, and I prayed through the flaking plaster with all my soul. '*Signore*, let me be a composer! Grant me sufficient fame to enjoy it. In return I will live with virtue. I will strive to better the lot of my fellows. And I will honour you with much music all the days of my life!' As I said Amen I saw his eye flare. '*Bene.* Go forth, Antonio. Serve me and mankind, and you will be blessed!' '*Grazie!*' I called back. 'I am your servant for life!' . . .

Peter Shaffer, from *Amadeus*

40 'Odd how He changes. When I was very young,' said Bruno, 'I thought of God as a great blank thing, rather like the sky, in fact perhaps He was the sky, all friendliness and protectiveness and fondness for little children. I can remember my mother pointing upwards, her finger pointing upwards, and a sense of marvellous safeness and happiness that I had. I never thought much about Jesus Christ, I suppose I took him for granted. It was the great big blank egg of the sky that I loved and felt so safe and happy with. It went with a sense of being curled up. Perhaps I felt I was inside the egg. Later it was different, it was when I first started to look at spiders. Do you know, Nigel, that there is a spider called *Amaurobius*, which lives in a burrow and has its young in the late summer, and then it dies when the frosts begin, and the young spiders live through the cold by eating their mother's dead body. One can't believe that's an accident. I don't know that I imagined God as having thought it all out, but somehow He was connected with the pattern, He was the pattern, He *was* those spiders which I watched in the light of my electric torch on summer nights. There was a wonderfulness, a separateness, it was the divine to see those spiders living their extraordinary lives. Later on in adolescence it all became confused with emotion. I thought that God was Love, a big sloppy love that drenched the world with big wet kisses and made everything all right. I felt myself transformed, purified, glorified. I'd never thought about innocence before but then I experienced it. I was a radiant youth. I was deeply touched by myself. I loved God, I was in love with God, and the world was full of the power of love. There was a lot of God at that time. Afterwards He became less, He got drier and pettier and more like an official who made rules. I had to watch my step with Him. He was a kind of bureaucrat making checks and counterchecks. There was no innocence and no radiance then. I stopped loving Him and began to find Him depressing. Then He receded altogether, He became something that the women did, a sort of female activity, though very occasionally I met Him again, most often in country churches when I was alone and suddenly He would be there. He was different once more in those meetings. He wasn't an official any longer. He was something rather lost and pathetic, a little crazed perhaps, and small. I felt sorry for Him. If I had been able to take Him by the hand it would have been like leading a little child. Yet He had His own places, His own holes and burrows, and it could still be a sort of surprise to find Him there. Later on again He was simply gone, he was nothing but an intellectual fiction, an old hypothesis, a piece of literature.'

Iris Murdoch, from *Bruno's Dream*

41　The Prayer of the Lark

I am here! O my God.
I am here, I am here!
You draw me away from earth,
and I climb to You
in a passion of shrilling,
to the dot in heaven
where, for an instant, You crucify me.
When will You keep me forever?
Must You always let me fall
back to the furrow's dip,
a poor bird of clay?
Oh, at least
let my exultant nothingness
soar to the glory of Your mercy
in the same hope,
until death. Amen

Carmen Bernos de Gasztoid

42   Echoes from a Distance

Today begin Sunday, I shall go to church
And listen to the words men say you spoke
In times gone by. We, in our turn
Will call upon your name
And give you praise and prayer
And say such things as we suppose
Are pleasing to you, Lord.
Thus we shall speak
Together, and to you,
Like friends
Beside a bed in hospital
Filling the silence —
The silence of the empty tabernacle
The silence of the empty tomb.

Our words fan out in space and time
Like multiplying ripples on a pool
With, at their centre, stillness.
We reach our limits and rebound:
Who now shall read the interference pattern?
Who shall describe the cause?

Which is more true
The pattern or the cause?
Can either be without the other?

Without speaking, what hearing?
Without hearing, what communicating?
Without communicating, what word?

Where can a word be spoken and be heard
But in an empty space enclosed,
Such as a tabernacle, or a tomb,
The formless space of God
Within a separated consciousness,
The sea within a shell of flesh and blood
An ear made to be silent
And a mouth to speak,
A life to be full filled.

W.S. Beattie

43 Spirit of Affirmation

I am the way that stretches out before –
I am the journey you are on,
I am the present moment that you tread –
I am the next place that you stand upon.

I am the air you breathe –
I am every part and of the whole,
I am the love you cannot fall beyond –
I am the inner silence of your soul.

I am the question that you ask –
I am the answer that you crave,
I am the reality of truth,
I am the ever-living thread that leaps the grave.

I am all time in now,
I am this minute to begin,
I am the one that you have always known;
I am the peace that you may dwell within.

Cecily Taylor

44 The world is charged with the grandeur of God.
It will flame out, like shining from shook foil;
It gathers to a greatness, like the ooze of oil
Crushed. Why do men then now not reck his rod?
Generations have trod, have trod, have trod;
And all is seared with trade; bleared, smeared with toil;
And wears man's smudge and shares man's smell: the soil
Is bare now, nor can foot feel, being shod.

And for all this, nature is never spent;
There lives the dearest freshness deep down things;
And though the last lights off the black West went
Oh, morning, at the brown brink eastward, springs –
Because the Holy Ghost over the bent
World broods with warm breast and with ah! bright wings.

Gerard Manley Hopkins

45 The Last Enemy

And He who each day
reveals a new masterpiece of sky
and whose joy
can be seen in the eyelash of a child
Who when He hears of our smug indifference
will whisper an ocean into lashing fury
and talk tigers into padding roars
This my God
whose breath is in the wings of eagles
whose power is etched in the crags of mountains
It is He whom I will meet
in whose presence I will find tulips and clouds,
kneeling martyrs and trees
The whole vast praising of His endless creation
And He will grant the uniqueness
that eluded me
in my earthly bartering with Satan
That day when He will erase the painful gasps of my ego
and I will sink my face into the wonder of His glorylove
and I will watch planets converse with sparrows
On that day
when death is finally dead

Stewart Henderson

46 Of Power and Might

I stretched my hand up to a distant star
And found, like grains of sand, a countless host
That circled into outer space, so far,
My mind in that infinity was lost.
What Power has touched each spinning star with light,
And held the surging waters of the sea,
And caused the earth to rest upon the night,
And blossom form on every fruiting tree?
Within man's face is mirrored God, the dove
Of peace has rested on his head; so shout,
Creation, at this miracle of love.
Our tears will turn to diamonds hung about
The stars and, freely choosing, we shall be
Transfigured in our immortality.

Francis Nicholson

47   Prospects of Glory   *(John 17.22-24)*

See the perfection of a single rose –
Then multiply it by each flower that grows:
Wonder upon the texture of its bloom,
Beauty of colour, form, and sweet perfume,
On earth behold its glory!

From lofty height gaze on a cloudless day
Upon a scene to take your breath away:
The awesome grandeur of the mountain peak,
The shining ribbon of the river's creek,
On earth behold their glory!

The colours of the sunset sky behold –
Pale turquoise streaked with roseate hues, or gold;
Clouds, silver lined; star-studded skies at night;
The smiling radiance of the moon's strange light;
Above behold their glory!

But how much greater will the prospect be
For Christians who behold the heavenly!
The Saviour willed, in His High-Priestly prayer
That such should His eternal kingdom share,
And there behold His glory!

Before He had the world's foundation laid
God's love was in His only Son displayed,
And that same love extends to all mankind,
Oh, what amazing grace, when eyes, once blind,
Behold His perfect glory!

Dorothy Bull

48 Glorious the sun in mid career;
Glorious th' assembled fires appear;
Glorious the comet's train:
Glorious the trumpet and alarm;
Glorious th' Almighty's stretched-out arm;
Glorious th' enraptured main:

Glorious the northern lights a-stream;
Glorious the song, when God's the theme;
Glorious the thunder's roar:
Glorious Hosanna from the den;
Glorious the catholic Amen;
Glorious the martyr's gore:

Glorious, – more glorious – is the crown
Of Him that brought salvation down,
By meekness called thy Son:
Thou that stupendous truth believed; –
And now the matchless deed's achieved,
DETERMINED, DARED and DONE.

Christopher Smart, from *A Song to David*

49 Magnified and praised be the living God; he is, and there is no
limit in time to his being.
    He is One, and there is no unity like his unity; he is
inconceivable, and his unity is unending.
    He has neither bodily form nor substance: we can compare
nothing to him in his holiness.
    He was before anything that has been created – even the
first:
but his existence had no beginning.
    Behold he is the Lord of the universe: to every creature he
teaches his greatness and his sovereignty.

Hebrew Prayer Book

50　A thousand years in thy sight

The way from Alpha to Omega is marked by sign-posts showing
where things took a critical leap forward and where boundaries into
new kinds of being were crossed. The key to the map was found
in Teilhard's own subject. Look, he seems to say, look at all those
dull bits of rock and fossil which most people hasten by when they
visit a museum. They are far more important to my arguments than
the products of historical time: spinning-wheels, sedan-chairs, and
all that sort of thing. When you put rocks and fossils in order along
the scale of time, you will find beyond doubt that things have been
on the move, are still moving, and are equipped to go further. The
time-scale is pretty long – some three hundred million years – and
if you examine the fossils at intervals of, say, a hundred thousand
years, you will find the differences, in them scarcely perceptible. But
if you observe the start and end of a span of ten million years, you
will find that 'life has practically grown a new skin'.

Vernon Sproxton, from *Teilhard de Chardin*

51 'You will never enjoy the world aright, till you see how a sand
exhibiteth the wisdom and power of God: and prize in every thing
the service which they do you, by manifesting his glory and goodness
to your soul . . .

Your enjoyment of the world is never right, till every morning you
awake in heaven: see yourself in your Father's place: and look upon
the skies and the earth and the air as celestial joys.

. . . You will never enjoy the world aright, till the sea itself floweth
in your veins, till you are clothed with the heavens, and crowned
with the stars: and perceive yourself to be the sole heir of the whole
world: and more then so, because men are in it who are every one
sole heirs as well as you . . . Till your spirit filleth the whole world,
and the stars are your jewels, till you are as familiar with the ways
of God in all ages as with your walk and table: till you are intimately
acquainted with that shady nothing out of which the world was
made: till you love all men so as to desire their happiness with a
thirst equal to the zeal of your own: till you delight in God for being
good to all: you will never enjoy the world.'

Thomas Traherne (1636–1674)

52 . . . The familiar valley beneath me was half blotted out with drifts
of mist, swirling like grey ghosts eddying and circling. Then, as I
watched this extra-ordinary wraith-like scene, the sun came up and
the mist dissolved into flying tatters, an army fleeing before the
conqueror. Nothing I had experienced before was quite like this. I
stood entranced. The early rays touched the gossamer webs that lay
like veils over grass and hedgerow – and they sparkled, diamond,
crystal, pearl. I stood without daring to move hand or foot, till the
sun had risen over the horizon and the last of the trailing mists had
vanished into palest blue. What I've seen is a miracle, I thought. It
will never happen again.

Eileen Elias, from *Straw Hats and Serge Bloomers*

53 **. . . in the true centre**

I heard God laugh:
And sunshine broke into a thousand thousand pieces
To plunge into the hearts of men,
Earth poured out her singing into mountain's crystal silences,
Trees pulled their ancient roots and danced for joy.
Flowers sang, birds and beasts understood
And stopped, in listening wonder:
Shuddered the old, old fears to vanish into living light,
And man, set free at last from all the weariness of doubt,
Ran to gaze up into the eyes of heavenly reason,
In the sudden knowledge that in the true centre,
Love breathes on life, healing and making whole.
God the beginning, God the victorious end.

Joan Brockelsby

54 What did you find in the fields today
you who have wandered so far away?
  I found a wind-flower, small and frail,
  and a crocus cup like a holy grail;
  I found a hill that was clad in gorse,
  a new-built nest, and a streamlet's source;
  I saw a star and a moonlit tree;
  I listened . . . I think God spoke to me.

Hilda Rostron

55   Teacher told us the Devil liked to see boys and girls do wrong so
he can throw them into the Pit. I thought wherever could this awful
hot place be, had never seen it nor its owner, and didn't want to.
Thought I would repent of my sins quickly – did so – and wished
I could die and go to Heaven straight away, before I did any more,
but it was not to be – I was to know a deal more of this old world
first, and its ups and downs.

I went home one night after one of these lessons. It was a night
with clear sky and hundreds of stars winking at me, and for all I
was so feared it was a bit of comfort thinking heaven was p'raps big
enough to hold every one on the earth. I went to bed and dreamt
of the great Horse Chestnut tree that stand to this day a few yards
from the door of this house, and that a ladder was set up it to heaven
– the top was lost in indefinite space, lit up with a dazzling brightness
– and angels a-going up and down, and I stood at the bottom but
felt I must not try and climb. Then I looked up and see the stars like
great windows, just as teacher said, and the saints looking through
them down on to the earth, all glorious in intense light. Such a vision
as could not be imagined. After that I was never so frit of the things
teacher told us. Not that I'm finding fault, they did their duty to the
best of their ability and belief, they hadn't only the ideas they'd been
reared with.

George Baldry, from *The Rabbit Skin Cap*

56   Lord, with what care hast thou begirt us round!
        Parents first season us; then schoolmasters
deliver us to laws; they send us, bound
        to rules of reason, holy messengers,
pulpits and Sundays, sorrow dogging sin,
        afflictions sorted, anguish of all sizes,
fine nets and stratagems to catch us in,
        Bibles laid open, millions of surprises;
blessings beforehand, ties of gratefulness,
            the sound of glory ringing in our ears
        Without, our shame; within, our consciences;
        angels and grace, eternal hopes and fears.

            Yet all these fences and their whole array
            one cunning bosom-sin blows quite away.

George Herbert

57   Why bathe in Ganga's stream or Kaviri?
      Why go to Comorin in Kongu's land?
      Why seek the waters of the sounding sea?
      Release is theirs, and theirs alone, who call
      in every place upon the Lord of all.

      Why roam the jungle, wander cities through?
      Why plague life with unstinting penance hard?
      Why eat no flesh, and gaze into the blue?
      Release is theirs, and theirs alone who cry
      Unceasing to the Lord of wisdom high.

      Why fast and starve, why suffer pains austere?
      Why climb the mountains doing penance hard?
      Why go to bathe in waters far and near?
      Release is theirs, and theirs alone who call
      At every time upon the Lord of all

      A devotee of Shiva

58   There is so much frustration in the world because we have relied
      on gods rather than God. We have genuflected before the god of
      science only to find that it has given us the atomic bomb, producing
      fears and anxieties that science can never mitigate. We have
      worshipped the god of pleasure only to discover that thrills play out
      and sensations are short-lived. We have bowed before the god of
      money only to learn that there are such things as love and friendship
      that money cannot buy and that in a world of possible depressions,
      stock market crashes, and bad business investments, money is a rather
      uncertain deity. These transitory gods are not able to save or bring
      happiness to the human heart. Only God is able. It is faith in Him
      that we must rediscover.

      Martin Luther King

59 Cactus and Caterpillars

I asked the Lord
to give me a bunch of flowers.

But

The Lord gave me
a cactus, ugly and full of thorns.

I asked the Lord
to give me lovely butterflies.

But

the Lord gave me
Hairy caterpillars, horrible and obscene.

I was shocked
disappointed
grieved!

After many days
suddenly I saw cactus burst into bloom.
Those hairy caterpillars also turned
into lovely butterflies
flying and dancing in the spring wind.

How unfathomable God's purpose is!

C.M. Kao

60

A humble form the Godhead wore,
The pains of poverty he bore,
To gaudy pomp unknown;
Though in a human walk he trod,
Still was the man Almighty God
In glory all his own.

Thomas Chatterton

61 Measuring

Suppose you opened up enough
to let in sky and sun –
turned out the fusty room,
chucked out hoarded priorities –
there might be room for
unexpected, overwhelming joy!

Well, suppose one millimetre –
that might even be enough
to start a crack,
it's said one snowflake
starts an avalanche.

Dangerous, you say?
Giving uncalculated goods?
Unweighed? Uncosted?
It's a risk, of course,
they might be wasted;
though on the other hand
an unaccountable joy could be
an unsought compensation.

Scales balancing
all you give
Leave no margin
for ecstasy.

Cecily Taylor

62 Unending creativity

Have you ever seen a finished picture? . . . To finish a work? To finish
a picture? What nonsense! To finish means to be through with it,
to kill, to rid it of its soul, to give it its final blow; the most unfortunate
one for the painter as well as the picture. The value of a work resides
in precisely what it is not.

Pablo Picasso

63 Mischief

In the beginning
God made physicists
out of nothing at all.

Now hold on
said the physicists
that's against a law.

God,
having not yet made Newton,
said nothing.

Then God made theologians
and became man
and joined them.

Oh no
said the theologians
it's one thing or the other,
God or man.

God smiled
and passed the bread and wine.

Finally God made philosophers
and died for them.

We've got you there
said the philosophers
immortals don't die - it's inconsistent!

But God,
having anticipated this objection,
got up,
packed away his shroud
and walked back into town to see some friends.

And then
just when he'd got them really interested,
just when they were running out of arguments,
just when it looked like he'd put them straight
once and for all

God made disciples
and left

But that's God for you,
always full of surprises,
never know what he won't do next

Wouldn't put it past him
just about now with the
physicists theologians and philosophers
thinking they've almost worked it out
to come back
and prove them wrong again –

even though
it's the very last thing
he's likely to do.

Godfrey Rust

We worship you,
We give you thanks

Lord God, heavenly King,
almighty God and Father
*   we worship you, we give you thanks*
*   we praise you for your glory.*

We worship you, we give you thanks

After his conversion to Christianity a former atheist was asked to describe his first reactions. 'Now at last', he said, 'I have someone whom I can thank.' Luci Shaw (*item 68*), and Joan Brockelsby (*item 66*), both inspired by creation, would have agreed, as would Buzz Aldrin as he landed on the moon (*item 80*). People, and even pets can be the cause of gratitude, as can 'the smell of tar which is newly laid' (*item 85*).

Some of our gratitude is inspired by the experience of those who are denied what we take for granted, 'I will never know the joys of seeing colourful flowers . . . I will never know the excitement of a ball game' (*item 86*), writes young Jean-Guy Forgeron and, sympathetic though we are, it reminds us of our own good fortune. Helda Camara finds his gratitude for God's creation morally persuasive: 'May your magnificence stop me being mean.' (*item 72*).

64 Te Deum today

God, with every breath, we join in the ovation to you
the greatest; we cheer, shout and applaud you.

Universes beyond sight and sound dance to your tune:
composer, arranger, performer; without equal before or since.

Forces beyond intellect, insight and imagination chorus
in harmony with mysterious voices deep down and within.

God, you perform solo, spotlit and gracefully:
applauding stars blaze with reflected radiance,
   all who bring their friends, cheer
   those who sacrifice most, cheer
   even all the critics, cheer.

East and west, north and south, audiences shout and stamp,
clapping loudly as you move everyone to sing
and shower their bouquets
on the only one who imitates you to perfection.

Christ, today you are in the limelight
son of God for ever and ever.

Your humanity gives us liberty:
our birth is honoured by your beginning
and our death by your discordant end
when you bring to their feet all who stay for the final act.

Though now you are with God in splendour,
we are together, our lives reviewed by yours.

Through your blood given freely
transfuse us with new life;

that we may remain with you
and with all who have gone before
to share your perpetual, timeless joy.

Tony Burnham

65 Te Deum of the Commonplace

For all the first sweet flushings of the spring;
The greening earth, the tender heavenly blue;
The rich brown furrows gaping for the seed;
For all thy grace in bursting bud and leaf . . .
For hedgerows sweet with hawthorn and wild rose;
For meadows spread with gold and gemmed with stars,
For every tint of every tiniest flower
For every daisy smiling to the sun;
For every bird that builds in joyous hope,
For every lamb that frisks beside its dam,
For every leaf that rustles in the wind,
For spiring poplar, and for spreading oak,
For queenly birch, and lofty swaying elm;
For the great cedar's benedictory grace,
For earth's ten thousand fragrant incenses,
Sweet altar-gifts from leaf and fruit and flower . . .
For ripening summer and the harvesting;
For all the rich autumnal glories spread -
The flaming pageant of the ripening woods,
The fiery gorse, the heather-purpled hills,
The rustling leaves that fly before the wind
and lie below the hedgerows whispering;
For meadows silver-white with hoary dew;
For sheer delight of tasting once again
The first crisp breath, of winter in the air;
The pictured pane; the new white world without;
The sparkling hedgerows witchery of lace,
The soft white flakes that fold the sleeping earth;
The cold without, the cheerier warmth within . . .
For all the glowing heart of Christmas-tide,
We thank thee, Lord!

John Oxenham

66 Step into Joy

Here is a day, a golden day,
Be lavish as you spend it;
New and bright shining after rain,
Immaculate with promise, yours for the taking,
Rare with fine gold, it will not come again.

Spend it in ecstasy of worship,
Sailing the wind, with sunshine, sea and rain;
By great hills, gorse and heather mantled,
Patterned with racing cloud, then sun again.

Pour out with boldness, walking in singleness and splendour,
Let flower, mountain, friend an altar be,
For every moment holds a joy for your beholding,
Each tear of dew a light that only you can see.

This is a day for you prepared,
Be reckless as you spend it,
Let no exalted moment pass you by,
For every fallen leaf bears your appointed pattern
And lo, no one, but seven rainbows span the sky.

Joan Brockelsby

67 On the sands

The day was bright, but I am melancholy
Hoarding the light and waiting for the dark
To reach full tide. Here steadfastness were folly,
If choice remained. Cramped at this post I mark
The little fish that play around my feet,
The beauty of the darkening sky, the drift
Of clouds, and ever-marching waves, that meet
Somewhere beyond my fettered sight. Now swift
Above them rides the white arm of the moon
Calling the stars to life, while all around
Our lady-mother's skirts, as now the boon
Of sleep steals over her, there is the sound
Of water lapping upwards. At my post
I wait. Not fearless. That would be to boast.

W.S. Beattie

68 May 20. Very Early Morning

all the field praises him/all
dandelions are his glory/gold
and silver all trilliums unfold
white flames above their trinities
of leaves all wild strawberries
and massed wood violets reflect his skies -
clean blue and white
all brambles/all oxeyes
all stalks and stems lift to his light
all young windflower bells
tremble on hair
springs for his air's
carrillon touch/last year's yarrow (raising
brittle star skeletons) tells
age is not past praising
all small low unknown
unnamed weeds show his impossible greens
all grasses sing
tone on clear tone
all mosses spread a spring -
soft velvet for his feet
and by all means
all leaves/buds/all flowers cup
jewels of fire and ice
holding up
to his kind morning heat
a silver sacrifice

now
make of our hearts a field
to raise your praise.

Luci Shaw

69 Glorious Lord, I give you greeting!
Let the church and chancel praise you,
Let the plain and hillside praise you,
Let the world's three well-springs praise you,
Let the dark and the daylight praise you
Abraham, founder of the faith, praised you:
Let the life everlasting praise you,
Let the birds and the honeybees praise you,
Let the shorn stems and shoots praise you.
Both Aaron and Moses praised you:
Let the male and female praise you,
Let the seven days and the stars praise you,
Let the air and the ether praise you,
Let the fish in the swift streams praise you,
Let the thought and the action praise you
Let the sand-grains and the earth-clods praise you,
Let all the good that's performed praise you.
And I shall praise you, Lord of glory:
Glorious Lord, I give you greeting!

Anonymous Welsh prayer

70 The milk float,
the poor man begging,
the staircase and the lift,
the railway lines, the furrows of the sea,
the pedigree dog and the ownerless dog,
the pregnant woman,
the paper-boy,
the man who sweeps the streets,
the church, the school,
the office and the factory,
streets being widened,
hills being laid low,
the outward and the homeward road,
the key I use to open my front door;
whether sleeping or waking-
all, all, all
makes me think of You.

What can I give to the Lord
for all He has given to me?

Helder Camara

71 In the beginning, God made the world.
Let us give thanks for all that God has made.

Think of a time when you saw that the world is beautiful . . .
Think of a sunset over the hills,
 or sunrise over a sleeping city.
Think of a running river,
 or stars shining on a dark sea.
Think of light flashing on a puddle,
 or of geraniums growing in a window-box.
Think of a time when you saw that the world is beautiful
 - and give thanks.

Think of a time when you found pleasure in your body . . .
Think of walking in the wind, or digging a garden.
Think of dancing till dawn, or climbing a mountain.
Think of giving birth to a child,
 or of holding someone you love.
Think of a time when you found pleasure in your body
 - and give thanks.

Iona Community

72 Lord
isn't your creation wasteful?
Fruits never equal
the seedlings' abundance.
Springs scatter water.
The sun gives out
enormous light.
May your bounty teach me
greatness of heart,
May your magnificence
stop me being mean.
Seeing you a prodigal
and open-handed giver
let me give unstintingly
like a king's son
like God's own.

Helder Camara

73 Dear God,
Sometimes I feel like an earth-worm,
I crawl on my belly and eat earth from morning till evening, and dirt from evening till morning.
And people walk by and say: Ha, it's only an earth-worm and they hurt me and trample on me with their shoes. And sometimes a magpie walks up and down all majestic in black and white, and he pecks at me and I have to slip away into the earth.
Why do I have to be an earth-worm?
Why can I not be a flamingo, or a mighty roaring lion, or at least a butterfly?
Why am I just an earth-worm?
Dear God, you did not ask me whether I wanted to be an earth-worm.

My parents did not ask me whether I wanted to be an earth-worm, or whether I wanted to be at all.
And so I am what I am, an earth-worm
'Til that moment when you, God, whisper into my ear:
Earth-worm, you are important! Without you there is no life, no plants, no vegetables, no animals, no people, no university, no government, no science and art and no magpies in all their academic glory.
What can I say to this, dear God?
I know what I say: I say, thank you, dear God, thank you indeed.
I am important.
But, dear God, I wonder whether you couldn't tell that to the magpies too.
Thank you.

Walter J.Hollenweger

74 We can never know what to want, because, living only one life, we can neither compare it with our previous lives nor perfect it in our lives to come.

There is no means of testing which decision is better, because there is no basis for comparison. We live everything as it comes, without warning, like an actor going on cold. And what can life be worth if the first rehearsal for life is life itself? That is why life is always like a sketch. No, 'sketch' is not quite the word, because a sketch is an outline of something, the groundwork for a picture, whereas the sketch that is our life is a sketch for nothing, an outline with no picture.

Einmal ist keinmal, What happens but once, says the German adage, might as well not have happened at all. If we have only one life to live, we might as well not have lived at all.

Milan Kundera

75   I think perhaps I was six. I was taken to a park in the evening to enjoy a firework display. It was summer. There was a crowd of people by the lake . . . Against the darkening sky, before the fireworks were set alight, I remember seeing these trees, poplar trees they were, three of them. It's very difficult to say exactly what happened because the order of this experience is of its own kind. There was a breeze and the leaves of the poplars vibrated, rustled. I believe I said to myself, 'How beautiful, how wonderful those three trees are.' I think there was awe and wonder, and I remember comparing the luminousness - that's a grown-up word, of course - the marvellous beauty, the haunting oppressive power of those trees with the artificiality of the surroundings, the people, the fireworks and so on. Oddly, I kind of knew that this was something extraordinary at the moment it occurred. It was as simple as that, just seeing these trees, but it was the event of my childhood . . . I knew then it was going to last. And so it has . . . What happened was telling me something. But what was it telling? The fact of divinity, that it was good? − not so much in the moral sense, but that it was beautiful, yes, sacred.

From *Living the Questions* (Edward Robinson)

76   Look to this day
for it is life
the very life of life
In its brief course lie all
the realities and truths of existence
the joy of growth
the splendour of action
the glory of power
For yesterday is but a memory
And tomorrow is only a vision
But today well lived
makes every yesterday a memory of happiness
and every tomorrow a vision of hope
Look well, therefore, to this day!

Sanskrit poem

77 Vulnerable silence

The music finishes.
It is the quiet of night
Broken by the ticking of a clock,
The hiss of rain,
The growling of a distant car.
The silence of this interval
Is not for doing,
Not for resting
But to wonder in;
A vulnerable silence
Given back to us.

W.S. Beattie

78 For quiet things

Thank you God for quiet things:
for drowsy birds with folded wings,
for daisies as they close their eyes,
and tunes that sound like lullabies;
for trees that stand so still and tall,
and snow that makes no sound at all.

Hilda Rostron

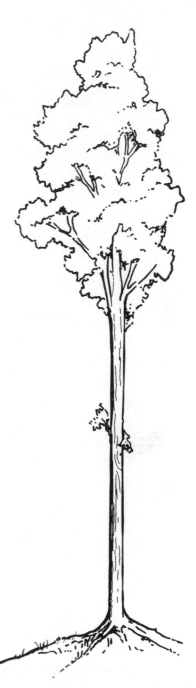

79   Prayer of the Butterfly

Lord!
Where was I?
Oh yes! This flower, this sun,
thank you! Your world is beautiful!
This scent of roses . . .
Where was I?
A drop of dew
rolls to sparkle in a lily's heart.
I have to go . . .
Where? I do not know!
The wind has painted fancies
on my wings.
Fancies . . .
Where was I?
Oh yes! Lord,
I had something to tell you:
Amen.

Carmen Bernos de Gasztold

80 Lunar thanksgiving

On the day of the moon landing, we awoke at 5.30 a.m., Houston time. Neil and I separated from Mike Collins in the command module. Our powered descent was right on schedule. With only seconds worth of fuel left, we touched down at 3.30 pm . . . Now was the time for Communion.

So I unstowed the elements in their flight packets. I put them and the Scripture reading in the little table in front of the abort guidance-system computer. Then I called Houston. 'Houston, this is Eagle. This is LM Pilot speaking. I would like to request a few moments silence. I would like to invite each person listening in, wherever and whomever he may be, to contemplate for a moment the events of the past few hours and to give thanks in his own individual way.'

For me, this meant taking Communion. In the blackout I opened the little plastic packages which contained bread and wine. I poured wine into the chalice my parish had given me. In the one-sixth gravity of the moon, the wine curled slowly and gracefully up the cup. It was interesting to think that the very first liquid ever poured on the moon, and the first food eaten there, were consecrated elements.

Just before I partook of the elements, I read the words which I had chosen to indicate our trust that as man probes into space, we are in fact acting in Christ. I sensed especially strongly my unity with our church back home, and with the Church everywhere.

I read: 'I am the vine, you are the branches. Whoever remains in me, and I in him, will bear much fruit; for you can do nothing without me.'

Buzz Aldrin, one of the first astronauts on the moon

81   The raw materials of love are yours -
Fond hearts, and lusty blood, and minds in tune;
And so, dear innocents, you think yourselves
Lovers full-blown.

Am I, because I own
Chisel, mallet, and stone,
A sculptor? And must he
Who hears a skylark and can hold a pen
A poet be?

If neither so, why then
You're not yet lovers. But in time to come
(If sense grow not duller nor spirit dumb)
by constant exercise of skill and wit,
By patient toil and judgement exquisite
Of body, mind, and heart,
You may, my innocents, fashion
This tenderness, this liking and this passion
Into a work of art.

Jan Struther, from *Epithalamion*

82 Helping hands

Praise be to God for helping hands
whose deeds say more than speech;
they lead, and bless, and mend again,
and in love's language teach.
Praise be to God for helping hands
begrimed and rough with toil;
they dig and delve, and plant and hoe,
in kinship with the soil.
Praise be to God for helping hands
whose action sings a song;
for holy hands with healing power;
these hands to Him belong.

Hilda Rostron

83   There are all kinds of men
     Who have done me good turns,
     That I still never think about,
     Not for a minute;
     Yet if I were making up
     That sort of grace.
     They would all of them have
     To be in it.

     One man made up stories.
     Another wrote verses
     I found, and I liked,
     And I read till I knew them.
     Another one saw
     All the things they had written,
     Then, being an artist,
     He drew them.

     Another took wood
     And a saw and some glue,
     And put each of them just
     In the place that would need it;
     So that is the chair
     Where I sit with my book
     And am so much at ease
     As I read it.

     I'm forgetting the one
     Who read tale after tale
     When I was too young
     To know letter from letter,
     And the other who taught me them,
     Till in the end
     I could read for myself -
     Which was better.

     Rodney Bennett

84　A very special present

A boy went to a shop one day
With his mum and dad.
The day was warm, the air was fresh
And Frederick was glad.
He was glad about all kind of things
Like circuses and fairs.
Chewing gum and lollipops,
And sliding down the stairs.
He walked right on into the shop,
An eager bright-eyed boy.
No games or toys or comic books
That others might enjoy,
But dogs and cats and kittens, too,
Mice, budgies, and a parrot,
And, all alone, a guinea pig
Munched quickly on a carrot!
Then all at once, a little pup
Tired of being 'on show'
Licked his hand with a warm pink tongue,
'This one's for me, I know!'
His parents, smiling down at him
Said, 'Yes', for they could see
The warm contented little pup
Completes their family.

Alison Campbell, 14 years

85 These I have loved

These I have loved:
The taste of hard crisp cornets,
The different colours of the summer flowers
    Intermingling with each other,
The smell of things which have
    Been newly painted.
Watching the rain falling from the sky
    When it is having races down the window pane,
The smell of tar which is newly laid,
Dropping a stone in a little pond
    Watching the rings getting bigger,
Running my hand across velvet and fur
    To feel how lovely and soft it is,
Smell of a pipe which has just been lit,
Arriving at the coast with the smell of salt and sea air,
The setting of the sun which lights the sky up red
    Which makes it look as though there is an
        island in the sky.

Janet Smith, 10 years

86 ... and I have not

I will never know the joys of seeing colourful flowers and the
blooming apple trees in spring. I will never know of the excitement
of a ball game or watching a circus. I will never know how it is at
a disco with flashing lights or the lights of the city at night. I will
never know how it is watching Scotty, my guide dog, playing in the
fields nor will I ever know the sight of the roaring Niagara Falls with
my family. These are some of the joys I will never know.

Jean-Guy Forgeron, 10 years

87   I would like people to know that 'What you've never had you don't
miss' is not true. I do miss not being able to ride a bike or skateboard.
I also miss not being able to do little things like splashing in rain
puddles or being able to ride on a double decker bus. I would like
them to understand what it is like to have to spend a large part of
your childhood in hospital, but I would not wish it upon them.

Heather Jones

88   With shame I press that paper

I am forty, or somewhere near, I'm told.
What I have learned is through my ears alone.
My eyes see only trees, the sky, my children, the food, my meagre wage.
In this way I am like all others – what is seen by them is seen by me – for all but one enormous thing – the words that people write and read.
These to me are but a bitter misery of mystery. When letters I must send, they are written by one child, ten, my son. God knows if he writes it as I say, or some nonsense of his own. My head was never schooled, only my hands, my back, my feet were trained to do the bidding of those who walk a higher path than me.
Deprived I was born, starved I will die, knowing nothing of any world but this, bounded by my unclean ignorance.
At the end of each stretch of thirty days, I take my pay and swear to it with one dirtied print of my right hand thumb.
Why this thumb is so different from any other will forever be my puzzle. It is with shame I press that paper, while those behind me laugh, for they take pen to hand and proudly sign a name for all to read.
Who can read a thumb? I vowed that never would my children live but half a life, and almost sooner than they walked I pushed them to a school.
There is not time now, at my old age, to learn to read what others tell, and content and passive I must remain, to see my sons rise somewhere near the sun.
I hope their skills will be reward enough, and when they walk their mighty road, they will take with them their mother in their hearts.

Margaret Duncan

89   Deaf people too should live in hope!

Hope! Whenever I hear that word, my heart starts pounding in my breast and feels like it will swell up like a balloon.
But I am abnormal, so I cannot join normal people. Most deaf people are frustrated in the face of hope and are leading desperate lives with bitter hearts. I want to shout, 'Deaf people too should live in hope!' This may be talking to myself. I don't know. People who have lost hope are like people who have lost their souls. I will live with hope even though I can feel my hope perishing like water bubbles.

Eun Seong Son, 14 years

90 **Assets – a poem for three voices**

'I have four big lollies.'

'Ten were given to me:'

'I will show you
where blackberries grow
if you'll come and see.'

'I have twenty fireworks.'

'I've got sixty-three.'

'I know a place
where the sunset and moon
reflect in the sea.'

'I can shout the loudest.'

'Just you listen to me.'

'I share a space
that is full of quiet
with a willow tree.'

'I've got the bomb and a country.'

'I rule over three.'

'I have the birds
and the curving sky,
and *all* that is free.'

Cecily Taylor

91　Undiminished in receiving

A child's first encounter with the hypocrisy of giving often comes with Christmas presents. Santa Claus, the child learns, does not scatter his gifts only to celebrate the joy of life and Christmas. He prefers *good* children, and Santa's notions as to what comprises goodness coincide exactly with those of the parents of the child.

Goodness a child learns, includes pretending to like the presents one gets. Childhood memories of Christmas are not just of joy and love. Children experience shame and humiliation when they fail to simulate the gratitude that is expected.

It is not just the young and the weak who are manipulated by gifts. Anyone who can be seen to be in a position to bestow a benefice, be it money, or power, or just acknowledgment, is showered with gifts by those who want access to that money or power. The principle at work is expressed in the old biblical dictum: 'Unto every one that hath shall be given, and he shall have in abundance: but from him that hath not shall be taken away even that which he hath' (Matthew 25.29). That is if you have nothing to give back, you will not be given much except perhaps advice on knitting your own woolly cap.

Giving to the haves has reached ridiculous proportions. The managing director of a company will get Fortnum and Mason's hampers, crates of wine, rare whiskies, cigars, and desk top toys, while the shopfloor worker will be lucky if the foreman stands him a pint. The cleaners just hope that a Christmas card to the staff will spur someone to give a few coins as a seasonal tip.

If ever Christmas is to become a celebration of life and loving, with or without the Christian message, we all have to learn to be undiminished when receiving gifts, or even ungrateful...

To be undiminished in receiving presents, abandon your belief that the recipient is put in a position of weakness. A gift should be seen as a communication between equals. The child giving you a present which he has made is honouring you by treating you as an equal. Your boss giving you a bottle of scotch is not.

If the gifts you wish to receive are those which come with the thought, 'I love you.' then you should remember that true love is always a gift freely given and should be freely received.

True love does not say: 'Because I love you you must do and be what I want.' True love says: 'I love you because you are you, and I wish you well, even if that "well" does not include me.' The gift of true love is the only free gift and the only one worth receiving.

Dorothy Rowe, *The Independent* 20 December 1988.

92 'When you grow up, Jakov − and let's face it, half the people in the world never do − you learn that there's always a bill to pay for being born. Nobody can pay it all at once, so you do it on the instalment plan − with interest. We all slip up on a month or two, or a year or two, but we're not very happy until the account is straight again . . .'

'And who pays us, Franz? For God's sake who pays us for what we spend and don't get back?'

'Nobody, Jakov. We're paid in advance.'

'With what?'

'With life!' There was a sudden fire in the old, wise eyes. 'Just with life − short or long, happy or unhappy. One breath of air, one look at the sun, one smile on a child's face, one taste of the apple of knowledge, even if it turns to dust and ashes in your mouth. Add it up man, and tell me honestly if you can claim you've been cheated!'

Morris West, from *The Tower of Babel*

We Believe

We believe in one God, the Father, the Almighty,
maker of heaven and earth,
and of all that is, seen and unseen.

We believe in one Lord, Jesus Christ,
the only Son of God,
eternally begotten of the Father . . .

We believe in the Holy Spirit,
the Lord, the giver of life,
who proceeds from the Father and the Son . . .

We believe in one holy catholic
and apostolic Church . . .

We believe

The ancient creeds were produced after long debate – and often as much to condemn error as define truth. Some churches have preferred 'statements of faith' rather than creeds, and have argued that, since Christianity is a developing faith inspired by a Spirit who will 'lead us into all truth', any such statements must be subjected to any change and alteration which increasingly knowledge and experience dictates. Albert Schweitzer's affirmation that 'faith has nothing to fear from thinking', is echoed in the recent plethora of faith-statements.

A worker's creed has come out of the political turmoil in Nicaragua (*item 97*). Feminism has given us a 'Woman Creed' (*item 98*). The One World movement produced its creed (*item 103*), and the 'Rainbow Covenant' (*item 95*) affirms new insights into the care of creation.

The ancient creeds centred directly on the Christ events portrayed in the Scriptures. Therefore, the second part of this section offers material which explores the life of Jesus from its announcement to his returning.

Creeds for today...

93 Paul vindicated for all time the right of thought in Christianity...
The result of this first appearance of thought in Christianity is
calculated to justify, for all periods, the confidence that faith has
nothing to fear from thinking, even when the latter disturbs its peace
and raises a debate which appears to promise no good result for the
religious life. Christianity can only become the living truth for
successive generations if thinkers constantly arise within it, who, in
the spirit of Jesus, make belief in him capable of intellectual
apprehension in the thought forms of the world-view proper to their
time. Paul is the patron saint of thought in Christianity.

Albert Schweitzer, from *The Mysticism of Paul the Apostle.*

94 I believe in God's World,
In beauty of earth and sky and sea;
In sunbeams playing on rippling water;
In moon and stars milking the midnight sky;
I believe in God's World.

I believe in God's World,
In green life pulsing through brown earth,
In miracle of bud and flower and fruit;
In great trees raising gnarled arms 'gainst rain and wind;
I believe in God's World.

I believe in God's World,
In cry of new born seeking the lifegiving breast;
In gnarled old age dozing in the sun;
In sweating brown backs bent over unyielding soil;
I believe in God's World.

I believe in God's World,
In the God-Man hung 'twixt earth and sky,
In the giving of one's life in the service of brother man,
I believe in God's World.

Gillian Rose

95 The Rainbow Creed

Brothers and sisters in creation, we covenant this day with you
and with all creation yet to be;

With every living creature and all that contains and sustains you.
With all that is on earth and with the earth itself.
With all that lives in the waters and with the waters themselves;
With all that flies in the skies and with the sky itself. We
establish this covenant that all our powers will be used to
prevent your destruction

We confess that it is our own kind who put you to death.
We ask for your trust
and as a symbol of our intention
we mark our covenant with you by the rainbow.

This is a sign of the covenant between ourselves
and every living thing that is found on the earth.

International consultancy on religion, education and culture

96 A new creed

I believe in a world meant for everyone
    to live together happily in.
I believe in living a life of love,
    sharing, and making friends.
I believe this is the way of Jesus,
    who makes me see my faults and my sin,
    forgives me and helps me
    to let him make me pure.
I believe he died for me and rose again
    for me, and for the whole world,
    and he calls me
    to join the people who follow him now.
I believe he can use even me
    to carry on his work in this world.
So I give myself to him.

John Hastings

97   A worker's creed

I believe in you, worker Christ light of light and true only begotten of God who to save the world in the humble and pure womb of Mary was incarnated.

I believe you were beaten, mocked and tortured, martyred on the cross while Pilate was praetor, the Roman imperialist, unscrupulous and soul-less, who by washing his hands wanted to erase the mistake.

I believe in you, friend, human Christ, worker Christ, victor over death with the immense sacrifice, you engendered the new hope for liberation.

You are risen again in each arm that is raised to defend the people from the rule of the exploiter in the factory, in the school.
I believe in your struggle without truce. I believe in your resurrection.

Carlos Jejia Godoy and Pablo Martinez, from *The Nicaraguan Campesino Mass*

98 Woman's Creed

I believe in God
who created woman and man in God's
own image
who created the world
and gave both sexes
the care of the earth.

I believe in Jesus
child of God
chosen of God
born of the woman Mary
who listened to women and liked them
who stayed in their homes
who discussed the Kingdom with them
who was followed and financed
by women disciples.

I believe in Jesus
who discussed theology with a woman
at a well
and first confided in her
his messiahship
who motivated her to go and tell
her great news to the city.

I believe in Jesus who received anointing
from a woman at Simon's house
who rebuked the men guests who scorned
her
I believe in Jesus
who said this woman will be remembered
for what she did –
minister for Jesus.

I believe in Jesus who healed
a woman on the sabbath
and made her straight
because she was
a human being.

I believe in Jesus
who spoke of God
as a woman seeking the lost coin
as a woman who swept
seeking the lost.

I believe in Jesus
who thought of pregnancy and birth
with reverence
not as punishment – but
as a wrenching event
a metaphor for transformation
born again
anguish-into-joy.

I believe in Jesus
who spoke of himself
as a mother hen
who would gather her chicks
under her wing.

I believe in Jesus who appeared
first to Mary Magdalene
who sent her with the bursting
message
GO AND TELL . . .

I believe in the wholeness
of the Saviour
in whom there is neither
Jew nor Greek
slave nor free
male nor female
for we are all one
in salvation.

I believe in the Holy Spirit
as she moves over the waters
of creation
and over the earth.

I believe in the Holy Spirit
the women spirit of God
who like a hen
created us
and gave us birth
and covers us
with her wings.

Rachel C. Wahlberg

99   The Creed of Liberty

Love alone is supreme
This I believe
And out of formless chaos did conceive
Purpose and design.
So came to birth
Fondly wrapped in loveliness
This earth.

God's very self, Jesus the annointed one,
Perfect revealer of God's face, Mary's son,
Lived in time and in recorded history
Dying a felon's death.
The mystery!
That Life itself should die to rise again;
Wholeness made whole in majesty to reign.
Thus through the light that is in Christ alone
The whole truth about us all is known.

The Advocate is with us when we meet
We are the Body of Christ, heart, hands and feet;
Forgiven, redeemed, together bound
Into a mystic fellowship profound,
Yet still myself, though I will come to be
Remade O Christ, and wholly one with thee.
This I believe, Amen I seek to say.
Help thou mine unbelief, Thou Living Way.

Phoebe Willetts

100 I believe in God, Mother-Father spirit
who called the world into being,
who created men and women and set them free to live in love,
in obedience and community.

I believe in God, who because of love for her creation,
entered the world to share our humanity,
to rejoice and to despair,
to set before us the paths of life and death;
to be rejected, to die, but finally
to conquer death and to bind the world to herself.

I believe in God who invites us into the community of the church
that we may, through faith and communion,
experience God's uplifting and sustaining grace;
that we may fulfil our human responsibility
and reach out for our neighbour;
that we may work to bring healing and wholeness
to a ruptured and uncertain world...and that we
may rejoice in the constancy of nature and the joy of life itself.

I believe in God whose word teaches us that the wheat and the
tares grow together; that the paths of life and death, good and
evil, too often converge...choices are not clearly defined...but
we confidently and responsibly tread the path we choose and
only God can be our judge.

I believe in God who is present and working in this world
through men and women.

I sense God's purpose in a spark of light here and there as
humankind struggles to keep a human face.
I know God's purpose as I watch children at play...hope born
anew in each generation...perhaps to be quickly extinguished,
perhaps to continue to burn brightly.

But for that hope I give thanks.

Norma

101   **Creed of Transformation**

I believe in God
Who didn't create the world as something finished
as a thing which has to remain the same forever
who doesn't rule by eternal laws
which are irrevocable
nor by natural order of poor and rich
experts and uninformed
rulers and helpless.

I believe in God
who wants the conflict among the living
and the transformation of the existing
by our work
by our politics.

I believe in Jesus Christ
who was right when he
'an individual who cannot do anything'
like ourselves
worked on the transformation of all things in existence
and perished doing it.
Looking at him I realise
how our intelligence is crippled
our fantasy suffocated
our efforts wasted
because we don't live the way he lived.
Every day I fear
that he died in vain
because he is buried in our churches
because we have betrayed his revolution
in obedience and fear
of the authorities.

I believe in Jesus Christ
Who rises into our lives
in order that we may be freed
from prejudice and arrogance
from fear and hatred
and may carry forward his revolution
towards his kingdom.

I believe in the spirit
who came with Jesus into the world,
in the community of all nations
and in our responsibility
for what will become of our earth,
a valley of misery, starvation and violence
or the city of God.
I believe in just peace
which can be achieved
in the possibility of a meaningful life
for all men
in the future of this world of God.

Dorothee Sölle

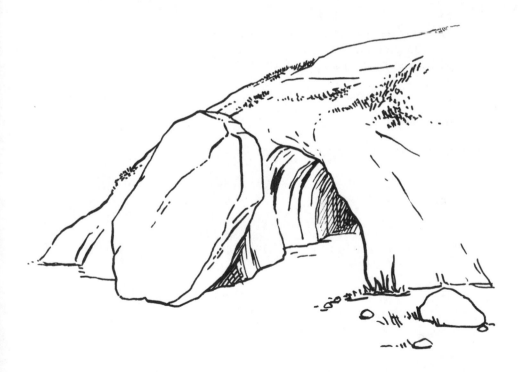

102 Father,
made in your image,
bought with a price,
recreated by love,
sustained by grace,
and led by the spirit,
we acknowledge our debt.

Father,
in your mercy,
you do not seek repayment;
in your goodness,
you make no demands;
in your eternal compassion,
you continue to give.
We acknowledge our debt.

Father,
your mercy begets love in us,
your goodness calls out our response,
your compassion invites our service,
and so, acknowledging our debt,
we praise you,
and serve your people.

Donald Hilton

103   One World

We believe in one world,
Full of riches meant for everyone to enjoy.
We believe in one race,
The family of humankind,
Learning to live together by the way of self-sacrifice.
We believe in one life,
Exciting and positive,
Which enjoys all beauty, integrity and science,
Uses the disciplines of work to enrich society,
Harmonises with the life of Jesus
And develops into total happiness.

We believe in one morality: love,
The holiness of sharing the sorrows and joys of others,
Of bringing people together as true friends,
Of working to get rid of the causes of poverty, injustice,
    ignorance and fear;
Love: the test of all our thoughts and motives.
Love: which is God forgiving us, accepting us, and making
    us confident under the Holy Spirit's control.

We believe in Jesus, and the Bible's evidence about him,
Whose life, death and resurrection prove God's permanent
    love for the world,
Who combines in himself life, love, truth, humanity, reality
    and God,
Saving, guiding, reforming and uniting all people who
    follow the way.

We believe in the purpose of God
To unite in Christ everything, spiritual and secular,
To bring about constructive revolution in society, individuals
    and nations
And to establish world government under his loving
    direction.

Subir Biswas

104   For handicapped people

They need to be helped.
They need to be loved by others.
They need to be respected.
They need to be considered.
They need to be educated.
They need to be trusted.
They need to be appreciated as useful people.
They need to lead a good, happy life.
They need to be fed.

Mwaniki Makau, 10 years

105 It is not true

It is not true that this world and its people are doomed to die and be lost –
This is true: For God so loved the world that he gave his only begotten Son, that whosoever believes in him, shall not perish but have everlasting life;

It is not true that we must accept inhumanity and discrimination, hunger and poverty, death and destruction –
This is true: I have come that they may have life, and that abundantly;

It is not true that violence and hatred should have the last word, and that war and destruction have come to stay forever –
This is true: For unto us a child is born, and unto us a Son is given, and the government shall be upon his shoulder, and his name shall be called wonderful counsellor, mighty God, the Everlasting Father, the Prince of peace.

It is not true that we are simply victims of the powers of evil who seek to rule the world –
This is true: To me is given all authority in heaven and on earth, and lo I am with you, even unto the end of the world.

It is not true that we have to wait for those who are specially gifted, who are the prophets of the Church, before we can do anything –
This is true: I will pour out my Spirit on all flesh, and your sons and your daughters shall prophesy, your young men shall see visions, and your old men shall have dreams . . .

It is not true that our dreams for liberation of humankind, of justice, of human dignity, of peace are not meant for this earth and for this history –
This is true: The hour comes, and it is now, that the true worshippers shall worship the Father in spirit and in truth . . .

Alan Boesak, at the *World Council of Churches, Vancouver*

106 To strengthen the poor

In penitence and hope we commit ourselves
to strengthen the poor against injustice

The majority of the world's people have scarcely enough
to keep them alive. They have little or no say
in what happens to them. Unlike the strong they cannot protect
or further their own interests.

We cannot be content to alleviate their suffering.
It must be brought to an end.
The world, we believe, is likely to be a fairer place where
strength is not left to take advantage of weakness
but is balanced by strength.

We must act strategically to strengthen the arm of the poor
until they can stand up to those who so often
act against them, and have the power to determine
their own development under God.

This strategy for justice is not ours.
We can only pursue it in partnership with the poor
and all who stand by them. We commit ourselves to
partnerships of mutual
sharing and accountability which try to achieve
in themselves the justice they seek everywhere.

As partners we will welcome diversity and make room
for disagreement. Differences of opinion will provide
opportunities for listening and plain speaking,
not occasions for parting company. Where however there is no
commitment to strengthen the poor
the future of any partnership must be called into question.

We believe this commitment, above all to a strategy for justice,
is required of us by our Christian faith,
which also requires us to look beyond a world that is fair
to a Kingdom that is more than fair;
beyond the power of the strong to strength made perfect
in weakness; beyond justice to forgiveness and reconciliation.

Christian Aid

107   Mission

Mission advertises God's love. It takes place under God's initiative, and finds its mainspring in the insights and message of the Bible.

It is the announcement which takes into account all we have experienced in Jesus.

It marks the rejection of all that separates, injures, and destroys, recognising that ultimately these things have been overcome by what unites and heals and creates.

It calls individuals and groups to witness to God who, furthering his purpose, encourages, calls in question, changes, condemns, and gives greater awareness, within all aspects of human experience.

It leads to personal and corporate growth as we reach towards the maturity we see in Jesus, and thus creates an openness to the perceptions of other Christians.

It involves a willingness to listen to, and be changed by, those to whom mission is directed.

It involves a commitment to working for a just and human society in every area of life, and in all the structures of society.

It respects the integrity of God's creation.

It is a call to people to commit themselves to Jesus Christ, and to share with his people in the life of the Church.

A Norfolk theological working party

108   This is the mission entrusted to the church,
      a hard mission:
  to uproot sins from history,
  to uproot sins from the political order,
  to uproot sins from the economy,
  to uproot sins wherever they are
      What a hard task!
  It has to meet conflicts amid so much selfishness,
  so much pride,
  so much vanity,
  so many who have enthroned the reign of sin among us.

  The church must suffer for speaking the truth,
      for pointing out sin,
      for uprooting sin.
  No one wants to have a sore spot touched,
  and therefore a society with so many sores twitches
  when someone has the courage to touch it
  and say: 'You have to treat that.
      You have to get rid of that.
      Believe in Christ.
      Be converted.'

Oscar Romero

109   If you have two pieces of bread,
  Give one to the poor,
  Sell the other
  And buy hyacinths
  To feed your soul.

A Hindu poem

110   The church's good name is not a matter
      of being on good terms with the powerful.
  The church's good name is a matter of knowing
      that the poor regard the church as their own,
  of knowing that the church's life on earth
      is to call on all, on the rich as well,
  to be converted and be saved alongside the poor,
      for they are the only ones called blessed.

Oscar Romero

111   I can't believe

I can't believe God didn't make the earth,
and when I think of miracles like birth
and all the marvels of a living cell –
I feel that something wonderful and good
must surely have created us as well.

I can't believe that Jesus never came,
and now it's known that someone of that name
was living then. The words we're told he said
are sane and living things that even now
shine out the truth that lights the way ahead.

I can't believe God wants the world to be
so full of darkness war and misery;
the thought that his own son shared in our pain,
and taught the way of love despite men's greed –
you'd think we'd learn from him and start again.

I can't believe that death is just the end
of all that our small brains can comprehend;
the friends of Jesus knew the answer well,
he gave them courage after he had died –
and we are prompted by his spirit still.

Cecily Taylor

112 Tell them they are loved

'And what's so desirable about originality, anyway? Sometimes it's the oldest and hoariest commonplaces that people see least clearly, because everyone who ought to be guiding the people is trying so desperately hard to be original! Common sense is common sense is common sense, men have owned it since men were!'

'Granted. Bear with me, Joshua, I'm not playing Devil's advocate for kicks. Go on, what else would you tell them?'

His voice dropped to rumbling, purring warmth. 'I would tell them they are loved. No one seems to tell them they are loved any more. That's a large part of the trouble. Modern administrations are efficient, caring, dedicated. But they dismiss love the way an insecure and weak man will neglect to tell his wife or his mistress that he loves her because, he will say defensively, surely she ought to know that without being told. But oh, Judith, we all need to be told we are loved! To be told you are loved lights up the day! So, I would tell them they are loved. I would tell them they are not evil, they are not festering with sin, they are not beneath contempt, they are not simple nuisance value. I would tell them that they already have every resource they need in order to save themselves and make a better world.'

'Concentrate on this world rather than the next?'

'Yes. I would try to make them see that God put them here for a purpose, and that purpose is to make something of the world He put them in, not channel their thoughts into an existence they can only enter by leaving this world, by dying. Too many people are so busy earning salvation in the next life that they only end by screwing this one up.'

Colleen McCullough, from *A Creed for the Third Millenium*

113 For the future

'In the year 2000 I would be 35 years old. But it is quite possible that I do not live so long. If I am alive, I shall be in Bangladesh, because I am Bengalese in every cell of my body. I have a close relationship to this country, its thought and its people, its water and land, and it is for this reason that I want to live in Bangladesh. Bangladesh will expect much of me. It is our duty to develop our country. If I am alive in 2000, my wish is that there should be only one nation, the nation of mankind, only one race, the race of mankind, and only one religion, the religion of humanity. I wish that there should be only one country, and that is the world, and finally that the whole of mankind can live together in peaceful co-operation and tolerance.'

Anawara Khan, 16 years

114

One day people will touch and talk perhaps easily,
And loving be natural as breathing and warm as sunlight,
And people will untie themselves, as string is unknotted,
Unfold and yawn and stretch and spread their fingers,
Unfurl, – uncurl like seaweed returned to the sea,
And work will be simple and swift as a seagull flying,
And play will be casual and quiet as a seagull settling,
And the clocks will stop, and no one will wonder
    or care or notice,
And people will smile without reason, even in winter
    even in the rain.

A.S.J. Tessimond

115

No generation has exactly the same mentality
as the generation that went before.
Christians have continually to appropriate Christian truth afresh,
not change but rethink their beliefs
and gain a new understanding
of the revelation of God in Christ.
That revelation is a reality always present.

Charles Davis

116   Elizabeth

My cousin Mary came to me today.
She is with child,
Yet she crossed the wild
Hill country
Just to be with me.
There was joy, beyond all reason, at our meeting,
And I take this for a sign
That between her son and mine
Will be a deep affinity,
Stronger than kinship's tie.
For now I begin to understand this:
That my bitter tears,
The long, empty years
And final despair
Were not a merely private affair.
Even in my fulfilment I had asked:
Why was our youth wasted?
Why could we not have tasted
This joy when we were younger
And blessed with strength and vigour?
I may not live to see my child full-grown;
But I will no longer speculate
About the future, I will wait,
Like Mary, upon the Lord:
Not in anxiety, but in peace,
Trusting His Word.

Susan Brown

117   Advent should admonish us to discover
in each brother or sister that we greet,
in each friend whose hand we shake,
in each beggar who asks for bread,
in each worker who wants to use the right to join a union,
in each peasant who looks for work in the coffee groves,
      the face of Christ.
Then it would not be possible to rob them,
to cheat them,
to deny them their rights.
      They are Christ,
and whatever is done to them
Christ will take as done to him.
This is what Advent is:
Christ living among us.

Oscar Romero

118 Mary

My heart is bubbling over with joy;
with God it is good to be woman.
From now on let all peoples proclaim:
it is a wonderful gift to be.
The one in whom power truly rests
has lifted us up to praise;

God's goodness shall fall like a shower
on the trusting of every age.
The disregarded have been raised up:
the pompous and powerful shall fall.
God has feasted the empty-bellied,
and the rich have discovered their void.
God has made good the word
given at the dawn of time.

Phoebe Willetts

119 Mary the slumdweller
Mary who longed for the liberation of her people
Mary who sang to God of the poor
Mary homeless in Bethlehem
Mother of the longed-for Saviour
Mary, exiled from her native land,
Mary, pilgrim with her people,
Blessed are you among women.

Noticias Aliadas, Adapted from *A New Litany of Mary,*

120 To many of us, reading or hearing the story of Mary is like reading
or hearing a story of which we already know the ending. We know
that Joseph is not going to abandon her and that he is not going to
throw her to the wolves. The penalty for a betrothed virgin being
with child by a third party was, after all, death. We know that
'everything is going to be all right'. Therefore there is not sufficient
awe in us at the incredible courage of this young woman, who said
what she said: 'May it happen to me as you have said.'

Marianne Katoppo , from *Compassionate and Free*

Birth . . .

121 Lovers remember places
then, just then and there
the first kiss, there in the orchard
under the apple bough
on that particular day,
pinpointing the universal
what is now
always and everywhere.

So faith sees Bethlehem
the time, the place
a stable where the 'Son of God'
assumed our state
eternal fleshed in time;
so we keep Christmas Day to celebrate
transcendent being which is love
is now and here
always and everywhere.

Kenneth Wadsworth

122 I saw a stable, low and very bare,
A little child in a manger.
The oxen knew Him, had Him in their care,
To men He was a stranger.
The safety of the world was lying there,
And the world's danger.

Mary Elizabeth Coleridge

123   We must not seek the child Jesus
in the pretty figures of our Christmas cribs.
We must seek him among the undernourished children
who have gone to bed tonight with nothing to eat,
among the poor newsboys
who will sleep covered with newspapers in doorways.

Oscar Romero

124 Sing high
Of son low
In cattle-crib
And candle glow.
Oh! Glory be!
Some shepherds see
Time nestle
In eternity.

Sing low
Of son high,
On grisly cross
Against the sky.
At Bethlehem
And Calvary
The finite
Finds infinity.

Johnstone G. Patrick

125 Each Birth a Revolution

Each birth is a revolution
whether it happened a thousand years ago
or takes place today,
with each birth the world becomes new.

Some are born in a cottage, some in a field,
but wherever a child is born,
in its eyes the world is reflected,
in its cries – Christ is present.

Christ the son of man
was born to renew the world
like every child in the mother's womb
is granted by the Lord at its time.

Sitor Situmorang, from *Children of Asia*

126   It had to happen some time.
How else to be reached
But through sinews and flesh – the very stuff of which we are made?
Within the creative span of human thought and the responding
human heart

To love as he loves?
Such close indentification with natural man staggers the imagination.
Such a profound compliment is breathtaking.

And yet, to think about it … a child is born.
Is not this the way it would be done?
There is a dead-end hope
that God is seen in idols,
in signs and mystic symbols,
in formulas of strict ritual …
What fools men are!

But this way …
Touching the very heart and mind,
And with full understanding coming to a knowing that there is no
other way.

Heaven burst open that awesome nightwatch,
And to see that dayspring old Abraham rejoiced and was glad.
That day when eternity snapped time,
And timebound men became the stuff of eternity.

Jim Moss

127   The 'flesh' is the concrete person. The flesh is we who are
present here – people just beginning to live, the vigorous
adolescent, the old man nearing the end. The flesh is marked
by time. The flesh is the actual human situation, human beings
in sin, human beings in painful situations, the people of a
nation that seems to have got into a blind alley. The flesh is all
of us who live incarnate. The flesh, this frail flesh that has
beginning and end, that sickens and dies, that becomes
miserable or happy – that is what the Word became. The Word
became flesh.

Oscar Romero, quoted in *Celebrating One World*

128 **You will find a baby wrapped in swaddling clothes...**

(Luke 2.12)

Such news was and always will be
incomprehensible.
The glory of God is a baby totally naked.
The longed for light that breaks
the darkness
is a child's translucent skin.
The hopeful voice that will summon the dead
comes not from the barracks, the capitol or the temple.
It is an infant's wail deep in a cave.
It is a total surprise, absolute shock and sheer grace.
The Mystery's name and Yahweh's claim is
vulnerability.

The only birth announcement
proclaimed in an empty field
to shepherds on the margins of life was
'Glory to God in the highest heaven'.

Maranatha, O naked baby.

Ted Schmidt

129 It wasn't that God (for this is what we call the Presence)
came down in Jesus but rather
through him.
We believe this Reality to be operative among people
of good will today.
And the reason we celebrate Christmas is:
A man, a Jewish man, was born long ago
and tore cataracts from corneal vision.
Unique, he was.
By his life, by his openness to transcendence
he taught us the lesson we celebrate daily:
The Universe can be trusted: We are not alone.
This Jesus we can believe in.
Isn't that a good reason to celebrate?

Ted Schmidt

130   Lo, Jesus came heralded by a star
       and so each year candles flicker
          and sweet carols rise.
What an infinitely small view man takes
     of this cosmic happening
        and spiritual intrusion!
God came to earth.
The Creator became a creature.
The Prince of peace became a pauper;
The Word of God a speechless child.
King he was in heaven
Yet on earth a lowly vassal.
The Source of all knowledge
thought the world was flat!
The communicator of truth
spoke Hebrew and Aramaic.
God came to earth
     to lie howling in his mother's arms
        and nuzzling at her breast.

And yet,
We sing sentimental carols
    of angel choirs
       and spotless shepherd boys
And wonder where
our God has gone!

Malcolm Hughes, from *Hiding Behind a Teacup*

131   Another Christmas,
      Another year ending;
      A year of pain and loss and bewilderment,
      Of beauty and fear,
      With a little love to make us go on struggling,
      A little joy to make it worth the struggle.

      Another Christmas,
      Another dream over.
      Do we dare to remember last year
      And the years before?
      So much is gone, so many memories,
      How can we stop what remains from becoming a shadow?

      Another Christmas,
      Another pause in the fighting.
      Can the pain that we give to others
      And the pain that we cause for ourselves
      Really be laid to rest by a Christmas card
      Or a sprig of mistletoe?
      Are we not as afraid of dying on Christmas Day?

      Another Christmas,
      Another pause for reflection:
      The morning I walked out alone in the cold golden sunlight,
      The evening I loved and was loved amid laughter and music,
      The afternoon of firelight and peace with my dream-shapes about me.

      Another Christmas,
      Another year beginning.
      Perhaps this year will see the end of us,
      Perhaps an indifferent stab will finally sever the tightrope on which
                                                      we struggle.

      Do we dare to hope for a new beginning,
      A new trust, a new wisdom, a new love?
      Is there even a possibility of a belief in Zion?
      We hear the old, old story
      ('A baby in a stable? How quaint.')
      Once more the road moves forward from our feet
      Towards a new Jerusalem
      And the shadow of a cross.

      Alison Head

132   Uneasy Christmas

I think about Christmas now it is near.
Our Christmas tree
All shining like a sunbeam.
But think about Africa:
They won't have fun this year.
The biggest present they hope to get is life.
I pray for them every night,
But it doesn't look like anyone cares because
There are no signs saying Feed the World.

But if you look at it another way
Everything is gay.
Everything is rosy.
Lights light up the hall.
Tinsel on the door welcomes everyone in.
The table has got lots of food on it,
Mince pies, an enormous turkey.
I go outside.
Lights on the wall,
Trees everywhere.
I go back inside.
The presents under the tree
All neatly wrapped up.
I wonder what they are?

It's lunch time.
I look at the table
And sit down.
But as I am eating my thoughts go back to Africa.
Sitting there dying,
Crying in pain,
Wondering what Christmas is all about.
The thought makes me feel sick.
Then I think about all the help they are getting.
Band Aid released their song again.
Last year it raised a lot of money.
But it's no use letting someone live for one year
If they are going to die the next.

Timothy Cook, 8 years

Declaring . . .

133   The Holy Child in the manger lies
Shown to the world through the Wise Men's eyes.
They offer their gifts in the stable cold.
Incense, myrrh and the finest gold.
Frankincense for a Child Divine.
Gold for Kingship, a royal sign.
Resinous myrrh, whose bitter breath
Speaks of rejection, grief and death.
Godhead, glory and suffering:
Strange are the gifts the Wise Men bring.

Love is our gold, our incense prayer.
Our myrrh, his sorrow in which we share.
Two thousand years have passed away,
The Epiphany rests with us today.
The stable is gone, there's nothing to see,
The world must meet him in you and me.

Katherine Middleton

134   'I may not sleep in Bethlehem,
Your inns would turn me back –
Because,' said Balthazar, unsmiling,
'My skin is black'.

'I may not eat in Bethlehem,
Your inns would frown me down
Because,' said Melchoir, uncomplaining,
'My skin is brown'.

'Alone I ride to Bethlehem,
Alone I there alight,
Because,' cried Caspar, all unheeding,
'My skin is white.'

Not one, nor two, but three they came,
To kneel at Bethlehem
And there a brown-faced Christ-child, laughing,
Welcomed them.

Mary Jeness, from *Opportunity,* Journal of Negro Life

135 The Four Wise Men

The first:
I bring the gift of gold; a symbol of wealth and glory; the standard by which the nations judge their prosperity and power. And yet the symbol, too, of human greed and selfishness. For this gift men have killed. On this gift has been built injustice and oppression. For this gift man has degraded man and woman.
With this gold I offer my hope – that human wealth and our resources may be used with fairness and with justice.

The second:
I bring the gift of frankincense; symbol of prayer and human aspiration; the silent longing that makes people lift their eyes to heaven; the inner power that draws us on from what we are to what we ought to be, reaching from our lowly origins among the beasts to stand in full stature.
With this frankincense I offer my hope – that people across the world will see the dignity that God has given us and recognize the rights of all.

The third:
I bring the gift of myrrh; symbol of suffering. Here is the tragedy of poverty, oppression and pain. Here, the agony of a mother who cannot ease her child's hunger; the father, who with strong hands, has no work to do; the family disrupted by homelessness and the country divided by war.
With this myrrh I offer my hope – that people will enter into the suffering of others and, in their sharing, discover a release.

The fourth:
I bring my gifts, too. The gifts of the twentieth century. For us, the possibilities of travel, the marvels of communication, news coverage and the speed of life have made the world a single place. The world is one world; able, if it will, to offer all its power and its resources, all its problems and pain in a common purpose.
I bring the gold of our industrial wealth; the affluence of Western civilization. I bring frankincense, the rising hopes of countless men and women across the world who are struggling to raise the standard of life, to find freedom from oppression and to establish the dignity of life in human rights; the hopes of new nations seeking true acknowledgement.
I bring myrrh; suffering; the cry of the poor and the refugee; the poverty of half the world; the growing pains of developing nations.
With these gifts I offer my hope – that in the gift of God in Christ, people's generosity to each other might find release.

Donald Hilton

136 The Song of the Magi

There is dignity here —
    we will exalt it.
There is courage here —
    we will support it.
There is humanity here —
    we will enjoy it.
There is a universe in every child —
    we will share it.
There is a voice calling through the
    chaos of our times;
there is a spirit moving across the
    waters of our world;
there is movement,
    a light,
    a promise of hope.
Let them that have eyes to see,
see
Let them that have ears to hear,
hear.
    But
look not for Armageddon,
nor listen for a trumpet.
Behold, we bring you good tidings of great joy:
The Incarnation.

Philip Andrews, from *Suffering and Hope.*

137 **'When King Herod heard this, he was perturbed and so was the whole of Jerusalem.'** *(Matthew 2.3)*

Herod had a right to be perturbed.
So does every Herod who sits on a throne of his peoples' bones,
and drinks his peoples' tears as unrighteous wine.
For coming to birth in Jerusalem
is a new Future for those on the margins of power.
The old arrangement will be no more,
and the One who whispered in Abraham's ear
and flared in Moses' face
will once more pull down the mighty from their thrones.
The baby's helplessness will prove stronger,
and Herod will be declared NO-KING.
The madonna's smile signifies something
only understood in Israel's blood.
Soon the hungry will be filled with good things.
Scream, rage and weep – 'no-kings', wherever you sit;
El Salvador, Guatemala, Pretoria, Moscow, Washington,
Downing Street.
Jesus comes,
and through us will build
God's kingdom of peace and justice.

Ted Schmidt

Living...

138   Christ became a man of his people and of his time:
        He lived as a Jew,
        he worked as a labourer of Nazareth,
        and since then he continues to become incarnate in everyone.
    If many have distanced themselves from the church,
        it is precisely because the church has somewhat
            estranged itself from humanity.
    But a church that can feel as its own all that is human
        and wants to incarnate the pain,
        the hope,
        the affliction of all who suffer and feel joy;
    such a church will be Christ loved and awaited,
        Christ present.
    And that depends on us.

    Oscar Romero

139   **Being shaved**

    I want to see the chairs that Christ carved
    And sit on a stool that He shaped
    When sawing and sharpening slain cedars of Lebanon
    or bending olive trees into tables
    Did He imagine the coming
    brutal bite of beam
    upon His back
    The ragged pole to which He would be pinned
    Glued tight against that wooden woe
    Malleted in place?
    He then slid off
    and cut down Satan's stake
    And as for me,
    Terrified at all my tawdry piety
    The Holy Carpenter
    now planes down my imperfections
    with chipped and spliced fingers,
    He bleaches the blemish of my grey grain
    And chisels out
    the sour knots that
    protrude and poison . . .

    This pure and practised Craftsman.

    Stewart Henderson

140 The Craftsman

In the beginning.
He just stayed close to his father,
Then his father taught him the names
Of all the tools –
Then he showed him how to hold them.
Then later as he grew stronger
He showed him how to use the different tools.
Soon he was able to earn a living.
His work varied from mending broken slats on donkey carts
To fixing shelves and doors.

His mind went back.
Over the last ten years or so.
And he remembered, with the true craftsman's pride,
The many boats he had repaired.
And how his work would continue to give good value
For many years to come.
He knew that some fishermen and boatowners
Had received a bargain with his work.
For himself, he was grateful to have always given good value.

He thought too,
Of the great heavy haulks of timber and planking.
That he carried on various jobs.
Sometimes he had wondered if the very sinews
In his arms would snap.
But somehow, praise God, he had always
managed to complete his task.
Now all that was finished.
All that remained, was to carry this cross
To Golgotha, the Place of the Skulls.

Bill Jones

141 Forty days

A journey lasting forty days
Through barren country, bare of shoots,
Still in the grip of winter's chill,
Where plants lie frozen at the roots.
Takes us, as days grow longer, and
The sun gains strength to melt the frost,
Onward towards Jerusalem,
Where one Man's death redeemed the lost.
Though all seems dead, the buds break through
And bright Lent Lilies nod and wave,
As from the gloom of Lent's dark days
He springs victorious from the grave.

Katherine Middleton

142 Jesus talked about the common things,
The bread a father gave his family –
The bird that is provided for and sings,
The money brought into the treasury;
He talked about the candle and the flames,
The salt upon the table and the fish,
The eggs, the oil, the light that went and came,
The supper for the hungry on the dish!
He talked about the sun, the fragrant flowers,
The need of trust in God our Father's will –
His watchful love through all the days and hours,
His faithfulness – His power our lives to fill –
He talked about the Heavenly Father's care
As if it were a thing so natural
To rest upon it and its blessing share –
That we should serve and love Him best of all!

R.D. Browne

143 The dreams of little people

All are to be sons of God. People used to call only the kings of Israel sons of God. But Jesus applies that term to anyone who is generous to his enemies. Everyone is then a king.

And is it not a privilege of the powerful to be able to give laws and repeal old ones? What does Jesus do? He defines new laws. He says:

> 'You have heard that it was said to those
> of old time,
> You shall not kill,
> and whoever kills is worthy of judgement.
> But I say to you,
> Anyone who is angry with his brother
> deserves judgement.'

Chuza had gone pale. He protested wearily:
'But why does he present his teaching only to the little people? Why doesn't he come to Tiberias? Why doesn't he teach Antipas? I can think of only one answer. He dreams the dreams of little people.'

Joanna agreed: 'Of course he dreams the dreams of little people. He's not addressing the rich and powerful. But what does he want to do? These little people are bent double by their toil. He wants them to walk upright. They're bowed down by cares. He wants them to be free from cares. They're people who feel insignificant. He gives them the feeling that their life has meaning. And you're all worried about that. All of you and Herod Antipas, you're worried that the little people might come to feel that they're not little people. So you've spread the rumour that you want to kill Jesus. So that he disappears over the frontier. So that he leaves you in peace. So that the little people don't hit on rebellious notions and become a danger to you.'

Gerd Theissen, from *The Shadow of the Galilean*

Passion . . .

144　When he came in sight of the city . . .

Dry not, dry not,
your tears of love eternal!
Only to eyes that fail to weep
does this world seem so dull and dead.

Dry not, dry not,
those long, sad tears of love.

Johann von Goethe
translated by Donald Hilton

145　The final barrier

Beyond the final barrier of all,
with deepening thought you gaze.
For house and home you have no further care,
For life and the dream of life,
– suddenly, all has gone.
Still, still you gaze,
With ever-deepening thought,
Beyond the final barrier of all

Peter Altenberg
translated by Donald Hilton

146　Mother Lord

And Thou, Jesus, sweet Lord,
Art Thou not also a mother?
Truly, thou art a mother,
The mother of all mothers,
Who tasted death,
In Thy desire to give life to Thy children.

Anselm, eleventh century

147 When tanks roll by and trumpets play
some people cheer and shout 'Hooray'
but Jesus chose another way
parading on a donkey.

He set out to impress them all...
a horse would make him proud and tall
and save him from the risk of fall...
but he rode on a donkey.

No soldier he, but King of Love!
The way he chose was well above
all hawkish ways, and as a Dove
he rode upon a donkey.

Folk must have laughed to see the sight,
a conquerer who would not fight
with what is wrong for what is right...
and riding on a donkey.

He had to show that he was brave
and that he only came to save,
Less like a king, more like a slave,
for he rode on a donkey.

No matter if the world despise
this Jesus-way of sacrifice;
for love lives on when all else dies;
and he rode on a donkey.

God offered love, not pomp and show,
so people everywhere would know
the way his kingdom has to grow;
so Jesus rode a donkey.

Who cares about the tyrant's pride?
Today Palm Sunday is world-wide
and millions stand with us, beside
the king who rode a donkey.

David J. Harding

148 'Next year in Jerusalem' –
And there you were:
But was it all as you'd expected?
Did you know the time?
Did you really know before the end
What the end would be?
Was there perhaps a half-formed hope
(as so many have hoped)
That 'next year in Jerusalem'
Would be the Promised Land
('If it be possible . . .'),
That the victory would be of a different kind:
A hero's victory, commanding
Amidst trumpets and shouting,
Not this strange ending, screaming
Amidst weeping and silenced.

When the crowd cheered,
For an instant,
The promise of a different messiah-ship:
The chosen one among the chosen people;
The easy way, loved by all.

And, as they left you, one by one –
Disillusioned, scared –
A desire to vanish from a dark garden
(' . . . take this cup away . . .').

So why did you stay?
What strength led you on to the end?
What faith made you face the faces
(' . . . not my will, father . . .')?

And, as when Prometheus gave us fire,
Were you there to suffer for us?
Or does your death speak of a different suffering,
Found in what it means to be human
(as you were human),
Found on the road to liberation:
A pain that leads to life?

Alison Head

149   A loaf of bread, a jug of wine, and a towel

The seed that's sown and harvested
Becomes this loaf of broken bread,

This loaf of broken bread that's food
For lasting peace and brotherhood.

The tree that's trained to yield this wine
Will tell of sacrifice divine;

Of sacrifice My friends will make
Before the Day of God will break.

My friends will never overlook
What happened when this towel I took;

For all that bread and wine may say
A towel will tell eternally.

Johnstone G. Patrick

150   Whose table is it?

Pastor Niemöller told the story of how people in the concentration camp asked if he would have a communion service with them. He told how he was puzzled because he was not in communion with all of them. With some, yes, but there were barriers of churchmanship, and he did not want to encourage anyone to break the barriers.

They asked again. Again he thought and prayed over it. He then told them how while he was praying it seemed as though a voice from heaven said to him: 'Niemöller, whose table is it? Is it yours or mine?'

He then said, 'I have never since then refused to give communion to any who come.'

Writer unknown

151 Was ever another command so obeyed? For century after century, spreading slowly to every continent and country and among every race on earth, this action has been done, in every conceivable human circumstance, for every conceivable human need from infancy and before it to extreme old-age and after it, from pinnacles of earthly greatness to the refuge of fugitives in the caves and dens of the earth.

Men have found no better thing than this to do for kings at their crowning and for criminals going to the scaffold; for armies in triumph or for a bride and bridegroom in a little country church; for the proclamation of a dogma or for a good crop of wheat: for the wisdom of the Parliament of a mighty nation or for a sick old woman afraid to die; for a schoolboy sitting an examination or for Columbus setting out to discover America; for the famine of whole provinces or for the soul of a dead lover; in thankfulness because my father did not die of pneumonia; for a village headman much tempted to return to fetich because the yams had failed; because the Turk was at the gates of Vienna; for the settlement of a strike; for a son for a barren woman; for Captain so-and-so, wounded and prisoner of war; while the lions roared in the nearby amphitheatre; on the beach at Dunkirk; while the hiss of scythes in the thick June grass came faintly through the windows of the church; tremulously, by an old monk on the fiftieth anniversary of his vows; furtively, by an exiled bishop who had hewn timber all day in a prison camp near Murmansk; gorgeously for the canonisation of St. Joan of Arc – one could fill many pages with the reasons why men have done this, and not tell a hundredth part of them.

And best of all, week by week and month by month, on a hundred thousand successive Sundays, faithfully, unfailingly, across all the parishes of christendom, the pastors have done just this to *make* the *plebs sancta Dei* – the holy common people of God.

Dom Gregory Dix

152 The benches were packed with Puerto Ricans, negroes, and Italians; among them men and women who would normally never enter a church: the drunk, the outcast of society. Just the kind of company Jesus kept. It is time for the prayer of intercession, and the minister asks, 'What prayers shall we offer to God today?' There is a pause. Then a Puerto Rican stands up: 'The landlord promised the Christian Action Group he'd fix the plumbing in Betsie's apartment. Signed the agreement too. We ought to thank God.' Another pause. Then twenty-year-old Josh is on his feet: 'Maybe we could pray for the families who'll be baptised next week?' Old Luigi rises, leaning heavily on his stick: 'Supposing there was another gang-fight like last night. I mean, just supposing' – The uneasy stir is broken by another voice. And another. Then: 'Let us pray.'

The pastor turns to the white communion table, looks up at the wooden cross that hangs on the deep-red wall, and then he kneels to offer the prayers of the courageous, the strong, the rejected, the weak, the despised: those who, together, are discovering how social and spiritual chaos can be fought and overcome.

Bruce Kenrick, from *Come out of the Wilderness*

153 I visited one of these banned people, Winnie Mandela. Her husband, Nelson Mandela, is serving a life sentence on Robben Island, our maximum security prison. I wanted to take her Holy Communion. The police told me I couldn't enter her house. So we celebrated Holy Communion in my car in the street, in Christian South Africa. On a second occasion I went to see her on a weekend. Her restriction order is more strict at weekends. She can't leave her yard. So we celebrated Holy Communion again in the street. This time Winnie was on one side of the fence and I on the other.

Desmond Tutu, from *Hope and Suffering*

154 Spontaneous sharing

An intriguing thing happened when BBC TV's first 'Global Report' documentary was being filmed. One of the programme's opening shots was of a hundred people representing the human family, standing together on a grassy slope. The hundred had been selected by nationality so there were a lot of Chinese and not many Swedes. Everyone wore national costume and brought representative lunches: the small group of Americans had before them a sumptuous, meat-filled picnic, while the larger group of Indians beside them looked sadly on their meagre portions of boiled rice.

What happened? Spontaneous sharing. The Americans invited the Indians over: the response was natural and seemed inevitable. No explanations, no haranguing – because the sense of community was there, of being one family ... Can what works in microcosm work in macrocosm?

New Internationalist

155 A black parable

Sitting around the table for the Lord's Supper are twelve Christians. Eight of them are coloured (black, brown, yellow, red, mixed race) and four of them are white. On the table there is rice, vegetables and chicken. Three whites (for there is also a small minority among the whites who are poor) and one coloured (the elite which co-operates with the whites in poor countries) start the meal by taking all the chicken, most of the vegetables and most of the rice. All that remains for the seven coloured and the one white are some unequal portions of rice and some left-overs, so that some of them remain hungry. After the meal, the remains from the plates of the three whites and the one coloured are thrown away. The rich also have wine with their meal, the others only the small cup of wine at the Lord's Supper which follows the meal.

Ulrich Duchrow

156   Lord Jesus Christ, Living Bread:
         vulnerable as bread placed in the hand,
         to be accepted with joy or cast aside;
         satisfying as bread to the hungry,
         and giving life for the future;
         broken like bread that all may share,
         and as necessary as bread to sustain our living.

     You are for us our bread of life

     Lord Jesus Christ, Living Wine:
         rich as the blood-red, sun-filled grape,
         taken, pressed, and destroyed, to new-create;
         welcome as the clean, fresh draught
         from the host to the visitor
         and refreshing the traveller on the weary journey;
         poured out in love that all may share,
         and gift to our thirst to meet our need.

     You are for us our spiritual drink.

     Donald Hilton

157   Did the woman say, as she held him for the first time,
     in the dark of the stable,
     after the pain, the bleeding and the crying,
     This is my body, this is my blood.

     Did the woman say, as she held him for the last time,
     in the dark of the garden,
     after the pain, the bleeding and the dying,
     This is my body, this is my blood.

     Well that she said it for him then,
     for dried old men,
     brocaded robes belying barrenness,
     ordain that she not say it for him now.

     Anon

158   Haiku Crucifixion

A cruel death, this.
Stripped naked, slow dying
body wracked with pain.

Palms shattered – throbbing.
Knees twisted, ankles fast locked.
Bleeding feet splintered.

Rib-cage stretched taut;
lips dry, tongue swollen. Reviled,
spat upon, cursed.

Darkness and great fear.
Faith shaken, God forsaken.
Grieving. Abandoned.

At the last, a cry
'Finished. Father in your hands
I place my spirit.'

Shaken the earth. Split
the stones. Twice rent the curtain.
Terrorstruck, the guard.

'Come down, save yourself'
they'd cried. Not so now. 'Truly,
Son of God,' they said.

Edith Purkiss

159   We who have loved – to-day we bring
Love's flask, filled full of ointment sweet,
And break it at Thy nail-torn feet –
Counting the cost, in terms of Spring,
A very tiny, trifling thing.

We who have fought – to-day we lay
The fallen flag, the shattered sword,
Upon Thine altar steps, O Lord,
Beside the victor's wreath of bay,
Commemorating Calvary.

We who have failed – to-day we hear
The broken echo of a cry
From a far Cross – *'Eli, Eli . . .'*
Before the skies are rent with fear
And Death becomes Life's victory!

Johnstone G. Patrick

160   I look upon that body, writhing, pierced
And torn with nails, and see the battlefields
Of time, the mangled dead, the gaping wounds,
The sweating, dazed survivors straggling back,
The widows worn and haggard, still dry-eyed,
Because their weight of sorrow will not lift
And let them weep; I see the ravished maid,
The honest mother in her shame; I see
All history pass by, and through it all
Still shines that face, the Christ Face, like a star
Which pierces drifting clouds and tells the Truth . . .
So through the clouds of Calvary – there shines
His face, and I believe that Evil dies,
And Good lives on, loves on, and conquers all –
All War must end in Peace. These clouds are lies.
They cannot last. The blue sky is the Truth.
For God is Love. Such is my Faith, and such
My reasons for it, and I find them strong
Enough. And you? You want to argue? Well,
I can't. It is a choice. I chose the Christ.

G.A. Studdert Kennedy, from *Faith, The Unutterable Beauty.*

161   The man who wants to live the life of a god on earth
must go the way
of every seed
and die before he has rebirth.

For he must understand what going this way implies –
to share the life
and destiny
of everything that lives and dies.

And like the smallest seed exposed to the sun and rain
he has to die
in wind and storm
before he comes to life again.

The grain of wheat can yield no harvest until it's dead –
it too must die
for other men
to be each others' living bread.

And this is what our God himself has already done –
he lived and died
as man on earth
to give new life to everyone.

Huub Oosterhuis

162 There was a scaffold in a courtyard of our prison in Dachau concentration camp. I used to look at it every day to receive its sermon. I had to pray a good many times because of it. It was not that I was afraid of being hanged on its scaffold one fine morning – one gets used even to this prospect as we all get used to the idea of having to die one day. No, what scared me was what I would do at the crucial moment. Would I cry out with my last breath: 'You are making me die like a criminal but you Nazis are the real criminals. There's a God in heaven and one day He'll prove it to you'.

If Christ had died like that, there would never have been a Gospel of the cross. No forgiveness, no salvation, no hope. There would have been no reconciliation on God's part; the Son of Man would never have been the Son of God. There would have been no new humanity bearing the very image of God Himself. He would simply have been in the presence of just another specimen of our race, this inhuman human race.

If I were to die like that, even in the name of Christ, I would die an unbeliever. Not believing that the prayer of Jesus prayed on the cross was meant for me too. For none of us can live by the grace of God, none of us can be reconciled with Him, unless by that same token at the same time we offer mercy and forgiveness to our fellow human beings. And, without the grace of God, we are of no greater worth than anyone else, even an SS man!

Martin Niemöller, from *Against Torture*

163 Mary's Guest

The pain of being over,
now I feel the sense of loss.
To see, to touch
caress and kiss
can never be the same
as when my body
was your home.
Then you were mine,
and yet not mine.
For when you stirred,
(although that was our secret)
I knew
the life contained within me
was not me.
You were my guest
my body housed your need
until it grew too great.
And though
a little while
I can sustain you yet,
the first painful
parting's done
from now
it is all partings.

From me you learn
to walk,
that you can be
the Way that
I may learn to tread.

From me you learn
the words
that you can speak
the Truth
that I may comprehend.

From me you suck
the life.
that you can be
the Living Bread
that I may feed upon
and live.

From me you learn
the love
which is the sword
that pierces my heart through,
and nails you to the cross.

In your necessity
my dearest dear
you were the guest
I entertained.
Now you are host
and at your table
I shall be sustained.

Rosemary Wakelin

Rising...

164 Messengers

It suddenly strikes me
with overwhelming force:

It was women
who were first to spread the message of
Easter –
the unheard of!

It was women
who rushed to the disciples,
who, breathless and bewildered,
passed on the greatest message of all:

He is alive!

Think if women had kept silence
in the churches!

Märta Wilhelmsson,

165 The dark doubts of the winter months are past
And Easter, young and green is here at last.
The April morning grass is bless'd with dew
And palest sun shines out of palest blue.
The old sheep stroll, the young lambs leap and play –
O, blessed is the lamb newborn today.
The withered root entombed beneath the earth
Puts out new shoots and joins the great rebirth.
The Spring is here, the egg, the grain, the seed:
And from them the imprisoned life is freed;
From Winter's cold grave, Spring's new life appears
And echoes his resurrection through the years.

Katherine Middleton

166   Reborn

Father
sometimes
I think
that
Easter
was something
that happened
only to Jesus
a long time ago
because
he had been so good
and perfect
but then
it dawns on me
that
Easter
is a gift
which you give away
to your world
so that
people
of all nations
can be reborn
and I
this very day
can come back to life
to serve you
in love
and hope.

David Jenkins

167 They were all sitting half dead in their wheel chairs, mostly paralysed and just existing, they didn't live. They watched some television, but if you had asked them what they had watched they probably would not have been able to tell you. We brought in a young woman who was a dancer and we told her to play beautiful old-fashioned music. She brought in Tchaikovsky records and so on and started to dance among these old people, all in their wheel chairs which had been set in a circle. In no time the old people started to move. One old man stared at his hand and said, 'Oh, my God, I havn't moved this hand in ten years.' And the 104-year-old, in a thick German accent, said 'That reminds me of when I danced for the Tsar of Russia.'

The script of a radio talk recorded in *The Listener*

168 Seven Stanzas at Easter

Make no mistake if he rose at all
it was as his body:
if the cells' dissolution did not reverse, the molecules reknit,
    the amino acids rekindle,
the church will fall.

It was not as the flowers,
each soft Spring recurrent:
it was not as his Spirit in the mouths and fuddled eyes of the
    eleven apostles:
it was as his flesh: ours.

The same hinged thumbs and toes,
the same valved heart
that – pierced – died, withered, decayed, and then regathered
    out of his Father's might
new strength to enclose.

Let us not mock God with metaphor;
analogy, sidestepping transcendence:
making of the event a parable, a sign painted in the faded
    credulity of earlier ages:
let us walk through the door.

The stone is rolled back, not papier-maché,
not a stone in a story,
but the vast rock of materiality that in the slow grinding
    of time will eclipse for each of us
the wide light of day.

And if we will have an angel at the tomb,
make it a real angel,
weighty with Max Planck's quanta vivid with hair, opaque
    in the dawn light, robed in real linen
spun on a definite loom.

Let us not seek to make it less monstrous,
for our own convenience, our own sense of beauty,
lest, awakened in one unthinkable hour, we are embarrassed
    by the miracle,
and crushed by remonstrance.

John Updike

169 Emmaus

Lifting to life
dreams three days dead,
we knew You when
You broke our bread.

Was it the way
You held Your head,
the word of grace
You warmly said,

or faith that found,
then understood,
bruised beauty from
a Roman rood?

Johnstone G. Patrick

170 It's darker now, but there is light within us;
We faced the sundown, yet our dawn has come.
Our heavy feet dragged on the westward journey
Which now are swift, for every place is home.

We came in sorrow, but in joy returning
We tread the same road, though with different eyes;
Hasten to share with others this new wonder,
Recall his promises that he would rise.

We did not know Him as He walked beside us,
Yet our hearts kindled at the words he said –
Slow to believe the truths we so much longed for,
But quick to know whose loved hands broke the bread.

It was the Lord, whom we had thought a stranger.
How dim our eyes! But now, with faith restored,
At any turn of roadway we may meet him,
In any stranger we may see the Lord.

Lucy M. Green

171   Come to us, Lord Jesus Christ,
come as we search the Scriptures and see God's hidden purpose,
come as we walk the lonely road, needing a companion,
come when life mystifies and perplexes us,
come into our disappointments and unease,
come at table where we share our food and hopes,
and, coming, open our eyes to recognise you.

Donald Hilton

172   The primrose
And the daffodil
Prime no ornate
Parade:
They come
In gentle colours
And in valiant hope
Arrayed.

They bear
Their Easter
Witness
For broken hearts
To learn
That after pain
In darkness sown
New life will still
Return.

A.J. Lewis

Returning...

173   It is not for us
to define the day
but he will come
and men will once again be called
to proclaim the word of God
in such a way
that it will change and renew the world

Dietrich Bonhoeffer

Holy, holy, holy

Holy, holy, holy, Lord,
God of power and might,
heaven and earth are full of your glory,
Hosanna in the highest.

Holy, holy, holy

There are those experiences in life that seem to touch eternal mysteries. Words fail to describe them; they can only be felt. Such mystery is 'a certain breath of wonder' (*item 174*), 'a sense sublime of something far more deeply interfused' (*item 175*), 'this present otherness' (*item 180*).

To describe is almost to destroy. Is this why, although Beth Webb finds that 'going to Church twice every Sunday . . . wears me out', she hopes to meet God 'in a flash of lightning' and 'praise him with a smile'? (*item 188*).

There is often an imperative within the moment of holiness, as when H.R. Williams on Easter Day experienced a 'merciless mercy' (*item 182*).

Fleeting though the experience of holiness may be, it is not infrequently associated with tangible objects. It is not only Romanian Christians during oppression (*item 189*) who found their church buildings to be a seat of holiness, nor only Anna Buston who, in a quiet moment, found holiness focussed under an apple tree (*item 183*).

Moments...

174   she almost saw it once in a rose –
a certain breath of wonder
she looked again perhaps that was her mistake
she should have gone on walking

and then again in mountain country
she heard an echo again
but it was muffled by thunder
and she had no ear for music

In the years that followed she found it again and again
in children that later got arrested on drugs charges
flowers that died, animals that bit her;
she almost had it by the hand in a symphony concert
but even the music faded

and when she finally found it (she was one of the lucky ones)
she found it in such a strange manner
it came up behind her and spoke to her
for a time she was frightened but at last she turned round

and it knew her, it loved her it spoke her name
it had always known her
it was amazing it was perfect
it was true, at last.

David Porter, *The Search*

175   I have learned
To look on nature, not as in the hour
Of thoughtless youth; but hearing often-times
The still, sad music of humanity,
Nor harsh nor grating, though of ample power
To chasten and subdue. And I have felt
A presence that disturbs me with the joy
Of elevated thoughts, a sense sublime
Of something far more deeply interfused,
Whose dwelling is the light of setting suns,
And the round ocean and the living air,
And the blue sky, and in the mind of man:
A motion and a spirit that impels
All thinking things, all objects of all thought,
And rolls through all things.

William Wordsworth, from *Lines above Tintern Abbey*

176 Summoned

Summoned
To carry it,
Aloned
To assay it,
Chosen
To suffer it,
And free
To deny it,
I saw
For one moment
The sail
In the sun-storm,
Far off
On a wave-crest,
Alone,
Bearing from land.

For one moment
I saw.

Dag Hammarskjöld

177   . . . there are times when I just feel the presence, if that's the word; it just happens. It's marvellous. It's terribly clear, but very hard to explain. It's practically always in answer to something. You try to get the answer yourself; you struggle hard, and sometimes you don't seem to be able to get through. You think all this is useless; I'm too tense, and at the back of my mind there are other things. You just have to relax, and concentrate. I can get into the state where I say it's just no good. And then suddenly, when you're not expecting it, you're through; the lines are clear, and you get a marvellous answer, absolutely vivid, enormously – I can't describe it – serene, enormous wisdom.

From *Living the Questions* (Edward Robinson)

178   Nature's scream

Geschrei or The Scream is Edvard Munch's most famous lithograph.

I walked along the road with two friends. The sun went down – the sky was blood red – and I felt a breath of sadness – I stood still, tired unto death – over the blue black fjord and city lay blood and tongues of fire. My friends continued on – I remained – trembling with fear. I experienced the great infinite scream through nature.

179   The silence of God

God's silence is mysterious. Sometimes it fills us with fright and paralyses us in the face of the devils who squeeze out the life of the people. But without this silence of God we can't become men and women. When God speaks all the time, people become deaf. They don't hear the cry of the poor and of those who suffer. They become dull; they no longer walk and hope. They don't dare to do anything. They no longer endure. God remains silent so that men and women may speak, protest, and struggle. God remains silent so that people may become really people.

Elsa Tamez, from *A letter to Job (New Eyes for Reading)*

180   Beyond the headlights

Driving at night
Along silent lanes
In the empty countryside.
Dim clouds, faint stars,
The distant lights of houses.

How simple it is.
There is this tree,
This hedge,
This piece of road,
This intimate circle of light and warmth.
Outside, the emptiness.

I am here the alien,
But drawn,
Probing this present otherness,
To recognise
Some further pole of being.

W.S. Beattie

181   Echoes

It comes as no surprise to hear Him speak
When the ocean breakers roar,
Or when the breeze plays in the sycamores,
Or when the stormy night growls.
But,
When I hear Him in the hubbub of the city,
Where distant relatives turn a deaf ear
And dance to a tune of anarchy,
Then I cannot help but thank Him for the unexpected word.
And a prayer within me rises up
Until it meets and mingles with my risen Lord.

Angela Griffiths

182   Merciless mercy

Easter Sunday came, and I thought I had better go to church, partly out of a sense of duty and partly not to upset John, for whom at that time (he is no longer like that) attendance at the Holy Communion on Sunday was a bit of a neurotic compulsion; all the more so, therefore, on Easter Sunday. So the three of us went to the small episcopal church in Lerwick. There were about twelve other people in the congregation at this eight o'clock service, and the priest was a youngish man attended by the usual adolescent server in his middle teens. We didn't discover to whom the church was dedicated, but for me personally it was quite definitely Trinity church, for it was there that I met my doom. The priest read the usual Prayer Book epistle for Easter Sunday, and a sentence of it burnt itself into me like fire: 'Ye died, and your life is hid with Christ in God.' The words overpowered me. It was like being struck fiercely in the face. Yet it wasn't like that either. For if the impact of the words was merciless, it was the impact of a merciless mercy. What pounced upon me was not so much a divine imperative as a divine invitation, though I suppose it could be said that these are different ways of saying much the same thing. Yet not always or necessarily. For what strikes somebody as a divine imperative may be a projection upon the heavens of his own pathological guilt-feelings. But an invitation, however compelling, is never compulsive. It has about it a supreme graciousness which frightens only because it attracts so mightily. From that moment I knew beyond a peradventure that I was being invited to die somehow to an old life in order to find a truer identity in the encompassing mystery of which I had been so long aware. In practical terms this meant leaving Cambridge and writing to Geoffrey Beaumont about the possibility of the Mirfield Community's being willing to give me a try.

H.R. Williams, from *Some day I'll find you*

183 Under a Wiltshire Apple Tree

Some folks as can afford,
So I've heard say,
Set up a sort of cross
Right in the garden way
To mind 'em of the Lord.

But I, when I do see
Thik apple tree
An' stoopin' limb
All spread wi' moss,
I think of Him
And how He talks wi' me.

I think of God
And how he trod
That garden long ago;
He walked, I reckon, to and fro
And then sat down
Upon the groun'
Or some low limb
What suited Him
Such as you see
On many a tree,
And on thik very one
Where I at set o' sun
Do sit and talk wi' He.

And, mornings too, I rise and come
An' sit down where the branch be low;
And bird do sing, a bee do hum
The flowers in the border blow,
And all my heart's so glad and clear
As pools when mists do disappear:
As pools a-laughing in the light
When mornin' air is swep' an' bright,
As pools what got all Heaven in sight
So's my heart's cheer
When He be near.

He never pushed the garden door,
He left no footmark on the floor;

I never heard 'Un stir nor tread
And yet His Hand do bless my head,
And when 'tis time for work to start
I takes Him with me in my heart.

And when I die, pray God I see
At very last thik apple tree
An' stoopin' limb,
And think of Him
And all He been to me.

Anna Buston

184   Let joy break out, eternal God!
Take the self-imposed blindfold from our eyes,
Rob us of the crutches we so dearly love.
Unshackle mind and heart,
And grant the freedom you have ever planned.
Let joy break out!
Throw open wide the gate to life
and help us find ourselves.

Let joy break out!
and flood our lives;
    creation spilling out its brilliant gifts,
    love finding itself lost in love,
    silence deepened, and all sound enhanced.
Let joy break out! And break again!
    as your fatherly love enfolds us
    as Jesus speaks the intimate Word
    and the Spirit enlivens our half-deadened lives.
Let joy break out! And joy again!

Donald Hilton

185   Late have I loved You,
     O beauty ever ancient, ever new!
Late have I loved You!
    And behold,
You were within, and I without,
    and without I sought You.
And deformed I ran after these forms
    of beauty You have made.
You were with me,
    and I was not with You,
those things held me back from You,
    things whose only being
was to be in You.
    You called; You cried;
and You broke through my deafness.
    You flashed; You shone;
and You chased away my blindness.
    You became fragrant;
and I inhaled and sighed for You.
    I tasted,
and now hunger and thirst
    for You.
You touched me:
    and I burned for Your embrace.

Augustine

186   Afraid! of Him?

Fastening their boat to a willow, the friends landed in this silent, silver kingdom, and patiently explored the hedges, the hollow trees, the runnels and their little culverts, the ditches and dry water-ways. Embarking again and crossing over, they worked their way up the stream in this manner, while the moon, serene and detached in a cloudless sky, did what she could, though so far off, to help them in the quest, till her hour came and she sank earthwards reluctantly, and left them, and mystery once more held field and river.

Then a change began slowly to declare itself. The horizon became clearer, field and tree came more into sight, and somehow with a different look; the mystery began to drop away from them. A bird piped suddenly, and was still; and a light breeze sprang up and set the reeds and bulrushes rustling. Rat, who was in the stern of the boat, while Mole sculled, sat up suddenly and listened with a passionate intentness. Mole, who with gentle strokes was just keeping the boat moving while he scanned the banks with care, looked at him with curiosity.

'It's gone!' sighed the Rat, sinking back in his seat again. 'So beautiful and strange and new! Since it was to end so soon, I almost wish I had never heard it. For it has roused a longing in me that is pain, and nothing seems worth while but just to hear that sound once more and go on listening to it forever. No! There it is again!' he cried, alert once more. Entranced, he was silent for a long space, spellbound.

'Now it passes on and I begin to lose it,' he said presently. 'O, Mole! the beauty of it! The merry bubble and joy, the thin, clear happy call of the distant piping! Such music I never dreamed of, and the call in it is stronger even than the music is sweet! Row on, Mole, row! For the music and the call must be for us.'

The Mole, greatly wondering, obeyed. 'I hear nothing myself,' he said, 'but the wind playing in the reeds and rushes and osiers.'

The Rat never answered, if indeed he heard. Rapt, transported, trembling, he was possessed in all his senses by this new divine thing that caught up his helpless soul and swung and dangled it, a powerless but happy infant in a strong sustaining grasp.

In silence Mole rowed steadily, and soon they came to a point where the river divided, a long backwater branching off to one side. With a slight movement of his head Rat, who had long dropped the rudder-lines, directed the rower to take the backwater. The creeping tide of light gained and gained, and now they could see the colour of the flowers that gemmed the water's edge.

'Clearer and nearer still,' cried the Rat joyously. 'Now you must surely hear it! Ah – at last – I see you do!'

Breathless and transfixed the Mole stopped rowing as the liquid run of that glad piping broke on him like a wave, caught him up, and possessed him utterly. He saw the tears on his comrade's cheeks, and bowed his head and understood. For a space they hung there, brushed by the purple loosestrife that fringed the bank; then the clear imperious summons that marched hand-in-hand with the intoxicating melody imposed its will on Mole, and mechanically he bent to his oars again. And the light grew steadily stronger, but no birds sang as they were wont to do at the approach of dawn; and but for the heavenly music all was marvellously still.

On either side of them, as they glided onwards, the rich meadow-grass seemed that morning of a freshness and a greenness unsurpassable. Never had they noticed the roses so vivid, the willow-herb so riotous, the meadow-sweet so odorous and pervading. Then the murmur of the approaching weir began to hold the air, and they felt a consciousness that they were nearing the end, whatever it might be, that surely awaited their expedition.

A wide half-circle of foam and glinting lights and shining shoulders of green water, the great weir closed the backwater from bank to bank, troubled all the quiet surface with twirling eddies and floating foam-streaks, and deadened all other sounds with its solemn and soothing rumble. In midmost of the stream, embraced in the weir's shimmering armspread, a small island lay anchored, fringed close with willow and silver birch and alder. Reserved, shy, but full of significance, it hid whatever it might hold behind a veil, keeping it till the hour should come, and, with the hour, those who were called and chosen.

Slowly, but with no doubt or hesitation whatever, and in something of a solemn expectancy, the two animals passed through the broken, tumultuous water and moored their boat at the flowery margin of the island. In silence they landed, and pushed through the blossom and scented herbage and undergrowth that led up to the level ground, till they stood on a little lawn of a marvellous green, set round with Nature's own orchard-trees – crabapple, wild cherry, and sloe.

'This is the place of my song-dream, the place the music played to me,' whispered the Rat, as if in a trance. 'Here, in this holy place, here if anywhere, surely we shall find Him!'

Then suddenly the Mole felt a great Awe fall upon him, an awe that turned his muscles to water, bowed his head, and rooted his feet to the ground. It was no panic terror – indeed he felt wonderfully at peace and happy – but it was an awe that smote and held him and, without seeing, he knew it could only mean that some august Presence was very, very near. With difficulty he turned to look for his friend, and saw him at his side cowed, stricken, and trembling violently. And still there was utter silence in the populous bird-haunted branches around them; and still the light grew and grew.

Perhaps he would never have dared to raise his eyes, but that, though the piping was now hushed, the call and the summons seemed still dominant and imperious. He might not refuse, were Death himself waiting to strike him instantly, once he had looked with mortal eye on things rightly kept hidden. Trembling he obeyed, and raised his humble head; and then, in that utter clearness of the imminent dawn, while Nature, flushed with fullness of incredible colour, seemed to hold her breath for the event he looked in the very eyes of the Friend and Helper; saw the backward sweep of the curved horns, gleaming in the growing daylight; saw the stern, hooked nose between the kindly eyes that were looking down on them humorously, while the bearded mouth broke into a half-smile at the corners; saw the rippling muscles on the arm that lay across the broad chest, the long supple hand still holding the pan-pipes only just fallen away from the parted lips; saw the splendid curves of the shaggy limbs disposed in majestic ease on the sward, saw, last of all, nestling between his very hooves, sleeping soundly in entire peace and contentment, the little, round, podgy, childish form of the baby otter. All this he saw, for one moment breathless and intense, vivid on the morning sky; and still, as he looked, he lived; and still, as he lived, he wondered.

'Rat!' he found breath to whisper, shaking. 'Are you afraid?'

'Afraid?' murmured the Rat, his eyes shining with unutterable love. 'Afraid! Of Him? O, never, never! And yet – and yet – O, Mole, I am afraid!'

Then the two animals, crouching to the earth, bowed their heads and did worship.

Kenneth Graham, from *Wind in the Willows*

187   'Enough!' said God. 'Enough. We have heard enough.'
'But have we heard the Truth?' said God's Son. He still had no idea what the Truth might be.
'No, not the Truth,' said God sadly. 'Not the Truth.'
'Then tell us the Truth,' said God's Son.
'What is the Truth?'
All the misty glowing shapes of the people on the grass were watching God, whose face now seemed brighter than ever.
'What is the Truth?' cried God's Son, insistent.
'The Truth,' said God finally , 'is this. The Truth is that I was those Worms.'
God's Son stared at his Father looking blank.
'And the Truth is,' God went on, 'that I was that Fox. Just as I was that Foal. As I am, I am. I am that Foal. And I am the Cow. I am the Weasel and the Mouse. The Wood Pigeon and the Partridge. The Goat, the Badger, the Hedgehog, the Hare. Yes and the Hedgehog's Flea. I am each of these things. The Rat. The Fly. And each of these things is Me. It is. It is. That is the Truth.'
God's Son remembered all that had been said about these creatures and He stared at the misty shapes of the souls on the grass, and under his gaze the shapes began to fade.
'Don't go away,' cried God's Son. 'Stay a moment. Did you hear all that? Did you know the Truth about all these creatures?'
But as He spoke they thinned, until they were no more than faint wraiths of mist creeping along the hillsides. And God's Son saw the oak leaves move, and felt on his cheek a slight chill of air.
He turned and saw that his Father had disappeared. Instead the sky was very bright under a long low cloud in the east. And the middle of that cloud glowed like the gilded lintel of a doorway that had been rubbed bright.
Then God's Son hesitated. It occurred to him, with a little shiver, that He was where He had wanted to be. He stood on the earth. And below him He could see the roofs of the farm. And there in the early mist was the village, and beyond it in every direction, other farms, where the people still slept, but where the cocks were already beginning to crow.

Ted Hughes, from *What is the Truth*

188   Excuse me God,
but religion doesn't agree with me.
When I pray and hold you precious
every minute of every hour,
going to Church twice every Sunday,
doing the right thing,
saying the right thing –
although I do it with all my heart,
it wears me out.

Dragging my life up to you,
I grow weird and weary.
I straddle two worlds
and succeed in neither.

Please God,
if it's alright with you,
may I just walk calmly,
common-or-gardenly,
not-very-holily –
grateful for your hand,
which does not always burn,
but always heals.

Sometimes we may meet in a
flash of lightning,
but mostly –
may I praise you in a smile?

Beth Webb

People and Places...

189 Every church is the most precious thing

Believers never have, and never will, be reconciled to the
    closure of churches.
We need to understand what a church is to a believer.
it is not just a building;
it is not even like one's own home.
Every church is the most precious thing in the whole world.
It is washed with the believer's tears.
With the tears of his father and grandfather.
Here he brings his loftiest feelings;
he was carried here as a baby,
and he will be carried out from here into the churchyard;
his parents and all those closest to him were taken from
here to their eternal rest.
And now insolent, thick-skinned, coarse people have forced
their way in here.
A believer who sees a closed, desecrated church feels as
though someone has spat,
not in his face
(that is easy to wipe away),
but into his soul,
into everything he holds most dear and sacred.

Anon
*Written in response to the wilful destruction of a Baptist Church by the authorities in
Comanesti, Romania*

190 The blessing of the God of Sarah and of Abraham,
the blessing of the Son, born of the virgin Mary,
the blessing of the Holy Spirit who broods over us
be with you all.

Amen

191 I AM, already

Before the missionaries came, the great I AM was already in Melanesia pioneering in our land to overcome darkness and destroy the forces of evil. People who came out from churches that were missionary-minded enabled us to discover Christ in our own context. Today Christ, through his in-dwelling spirit in us as Melanesian, is no longer white with blue eyes, but black with brown eyes. He does not only speak English, German, Latin or French, but speaks our languages. How easy then for us to find and discover Christ.

Our churches today must no longer wait to be ministered to. Our Churches today must not wait for handouts. With Christ we are challenged to be in mission to every person in every place, in every situation, beginning from where we are.

Albert Burua

192 Called to something smaller

We are not ordaining you to ministry; that happened at your baptism.
We are not ordaining you to be a caring person; you are already called to that.
We are not ordaining you to serve the Church in committees, activities, organisation; that is already implied in your membership.
We are not ordaining you to become involved in social issues, ecology, race, politics, revolution, for that is laid upon every Christian.
We are ordaining you to something smaller and less spectacular:
  to read and interpret those sacred stories of our community, so that they speak a word to people today; to remember and practise those rituals and rights of meaning that in their poetry address man at the level where change operates; to foster in community through word and sacrament that encounter with truth which will set men and women free to minister as the body of Christ.
We are ordaining you to the ministry of the word and sacraments and pastoral care.
God grant you grace not to betray but uphold it, not to deny but affirm it, through Jesus Christ our Lord.

Methodist Church in Singapore

193   Heaven and earth are full of your glory

The human race of the twentieth century
   has climbed to the moon,
has uncovered the secret of the atom,
   and what else may it not discover?
The Lord's command is fulfilled:
   subdue the earth!*
But the absolute human dominion over the earth
   will be what is proclaimed today:
bringing all things of heaven and earth together
   in Christ.
Then humanity hallowed will put under God's reign
   this world, which is now the slave of sin,
and set it at the feet of Christ,
   and Christ at the feet of God.
This is the bringing together that was God's design
   before the world existed.
And when history comes to its end,
   this will be God's fulfillment:
Christ,
   the summary of all things.
All that history has been,
   all that we do ourselves.
good or bad,
   will be measured by God's design;
and there will remain only those who have laboured
   to put things under Christ's rule.
All that has tried to rebel against God's plan in Christ
   is false.
It will not last;
   it will be for history's waste heap.

Oscar Romero
*Genesis 1.28.

194   Transcendence

Not for three months, let alone nine
Could Mary conceal His presence –
Nor was Joseph kept in the dark
Before His eruption like the morning star
At midnight breaking in winter –
He dazzled both shepherds and wise men:
We twelve were all blinded – three years –
Till flesh failed to veil Him, even from us,
In a calm stilled sea, and on one mountain top.
How then could we conspire to cover Him
With heavy human robes – bury Him
In puny feudal powers? Him,
Whose setting the sun mourned,
Whose light Death could not extinguish?
He burst out of that grave, propelled
By resurrection – casting us all before Him
By the blaze of His uprising.

Veronica Popescu

195   All that matters is to be at one with the living God
to be a creature in the house of the God of Life.

Like a cat asleep on a chair
at peace, in peace
and at one with the master of the house, with the
    mistress,
at home, at home in the house of the living,
sleeping on the hearth, and yawning before the fire.

Sleeping on the hearth of the living world
yawning at home before the fire of life
feeling the presence of the living God
like a great reassurance
a deep calm in the heart
a presence
as of a master sitting at the board
in his own and greater being,
in the house of life.

D.H. Lawrence

196   First Sight

When was it
that we first glimpsed God?
Was it in the
red, wrinkled smallness
in the half light?
Or later in the strong feet
striding across hills
which a few aeons ago
he had called into being?
Or with a strange thrill
in the hand which
reached out to touch some
indescribable deformity
and make it whole?
Or in a sudden contact
with those searching eyes,
splitting men's hearts like pea-pods
to pour in?
Or was it yesterday
when in a moment
of forgetfulness
we lost ourselves
and came across him
unexpectedly
everywhere?

Lynette Bishop

Blessed is he who comes

Blessed is he who comes in the name
of the Lord

Hosanna in the highest.

Blessed is he who comes

Most of them failed to recognise the long-expected Christ as he entered Jerusalem on an unexpected donkey. Only a few could sing their hymn of praise, 'Blessings on him who comes as king in the name of the Lord!' He still comes. Too often we still fail to recognise him.

For Jaini Bi, in desperate hunger, he came as 'two hundred grams of gruel' (*item 198*). Similarly, for Rabindranath Tagore he is 'where the farmer is tilling the hard ground.' (*item 201*) Oscar Romero believes that he comes 'as long as there is one baptised person' (*item 204*) and the Isalotto Community finds his word 'presented to us by our children' (*item 209*). He comes as a stranger 'piercing our ignorance with insights', (*item 218*) and for a dying Roman Catholic he came as a Jewish Rabbi. (*item 220*) A nurse finds him in hospital (*item 217*), and for Essop Patel he comes in revolution (*item 207*), whilst for Irina Ratushinskaya he is a hand pushing a couple of cubes of butter through a prison fence (*item 206*).

**197 John declared: Someone is coming...
to baptise you with the Holy Spirit and fire**

(Luke 3.16)

We wait for something, someone
to light our twentieth century night of death
to redeem the seventy-eight million who died
to keep the world safe for democracy
(and profit and control)
We wait for the birth of the one
who will stay the final anointing of cinder and ash,
who will make it all new,
transform our lives,
heal our necrophilia.
We can no longer abide the official optimism of the aged cheerleader,
of those who invoke the bigger pie,
the bootstraps pulled up,
There are no tears here, nothing of solidarity or hope,
no understanding of the view from the edge.
There is no realisation that the kingdom-bringer
waits in the virgin womb, ripe
to burst forth with liberty for the captives.
It is rumoured that thrones will be upended
and every Caesar stands on a banana skin.
The circus of the great reversals is set to commence.
Christos, the holy one of God will never play Sun City,
bless the silos, wear the military tunic
or sanctify the empire.
He will offer a new heaven and a new earth
and to toast his Christmas arrival
you must also dance at his Friday coronation.
Emmanuel, come warm our global stable with Spirit fire.

Ted Schmidt

198 Every noon at twelve
In the blazing heat
God comes to me
In the form of
Two hundred grams of gruel.

I know him in every grain
I taste him in every lick.
I commune with him as I gulp
For he keeps me alive, with
Two hundred grams of gruel.

I wait till next day noon
and now know he'd come;
I can hope to live one day more
For you made God to come to me as
Two hundred grams of gruel.

I know now that God loves me –
Not until you made it possible.
Now I know what you're speaking about
For God so loves this world
That he gives his beloved Son
Every noon through YOU.

Jaini Bi

*In 1973 Chitapur's famine-stricken people received substantial aid when
this poem was printed*

199 We were in a town filming and we hadn't anything to eat. Somebody
told us where we could get something. If you've got money there
is food you can buy.

So we went to this place and had a Coca Cola and a little bread
roll each. We were just about to start eating when in the doorway
there must have been about fifty or sixty people. You know, children
looking with big, wide eyes, an old man who fell on his knees and
came shuffling into the cafe, and started kissing my feet. The idea
of actually eating that bread roll, I mean, I would have been sick on
the spot.

Instinctively, you start breaking the bread into tiny, little pieces,
which isn't going to help anybody, and start giving to people – and
hundreds more come clustering round the doorway.

Michael Buerk *in a film report from Ethiopia*

200 In Brazil I sat with a woman – a mother – on a bare hillside. She and her people have lost almost all of their land. Nothing would grow on this woman's hillside. There was one dirty stream at the bottom of the hill with a few fish, otherwise there was nothing to eat. Two yards in front of where we sat was a small circle of wooden crosses. It was where she buried her children, beneath the dust. She had no food or medicine to keep them alive.

The parable of the sheep and the goats suggests that God is like that woman; that when I think of God, I should think of praying and turning to someone like her. What shall I offer such a God when I come to worship? And what shall I expect such a God to do for me when I am frightened and in trouble? And when I pray, what shall I say to such a God – this woman who has nothing at all?

I sat beside her as part of a world that crucifies her and shuts her out – that refuses to stretch out its hand to feed her and clothe her and visit her, or comfort her children. Yet, like the crucified, her arms are open wide in welcome. She greets me as a friend. She offers to share what she has, and she thanks me for coming.

That is the Advent God who came in Jesus of Nazareth. That is Emmanuel, God with us, forever empty and forever full – who comes and comes again in the poorest of the poor.

Michael Taylor

201 Open your eyes and see . . .
God is there where the farmer is tilling the hard ground
and where the labourer is breaking stones.
He is with them in the sun and the rain
and his garment is covered with dust.
Put off your holy cloak
and like him come down onto the dusty soil.

Rabindranath Tagore, from *The Hidden God*

202 O God, who lives in the slums, where the sewage runs down
the back of the houses;
where the mud walls crumble when the monsoon comes;
where rain soaks through the holes in roofs –
   help us to know you.

O God, who crouches at church gates, where people walk by
after morning worship;
whose name is beggar, cripple, leper, pavement-dweller –
   help us to know you.

O God, who lives in the outcaste street, whose children work to
clear off debt;
who hungers because you are unemployed;
who despairs because children starve and women suffer –
   help us to know you.

O God, who lies down to die under the bridge in the city,
covered in a rag as the traffic roars by,
whose body is carted away by the municipal sweepers
because all have forsaken you –
   help us to know you.

O God, slum-dweller, beggar, cripple, leper –
O God, without work, hungry, thirsty –
O God, forsaken, alone –
   help us to know you.

Timothy J. Mark

203 You are the God of the poor
The human and humble God
The God that sweats in the street
The God of the worn and leathery face
That is why I speak to you
In the way my people speak
Because you are the God the worker
Christ the labourer.

From One Voice

204   If some day they take the radio station away from us,
      if they close down our newspaper,
      if they don't let us speak,
      if they kill all the priests and the bishop too,
      and you are left, a people without priests
      each one of you must be God's microphone,
      each one of you must be a messenger,
      a prophet.
      The church will always exist
      as long as there is one baptized person.
      And that one baptized person who is left in the world
      is responsible before the world for holding aloft
      the banner of the Lord's truth
      and of his divine justice.

      Oscar Romero

205   A church that doesn't provoke any crises,
      a gospel that doesn't unsettle,
      a word of God that doesn't get under anyone's skin,
      a word of God that doesn't touch the real sin
         of the society in which it is being proclaimed,
      what gospel is that?
      Very nice, pious considerations
         that don't bother anyone,
      that's the way many would like preaching to be.
      Those preachers who avoid every thorny matter
         so as not to be harassed,
         so as not to have conflicts and difficulties,
      do not light up the world they live in.
      They don't have Peter's courage, who told that crowd
      where the bloodstained hands still were
      that had killed Christ:
         'You killed him!'*
      Even though the charge could cost him his life as well,
         he made it.
      The gospel is courageous;
      it's the good news
         of him who came to take away the world's sins.

      Oscar Romero

      *Acts 2.23

206   The last day of the hunger strike brought us a surprise. A group of
women from the hospital zone was brought to weed and hoe the
'forbidden' strip. We were on opposite sides of the barbed wire, but
eyed each other with covert interest. They were not allowed to talk
to us, and we made no attempt at conversation, not wishing to get
them into trouble. And then, quite unexpectedly, two of them stepped
right up to the wire when the patrolling warder was at the far end
of the strip.
    'Hey, girls!'
    We moved over to them. Quickly-quickly they pulled out a couple
of small parcels from under their uniform smocks, thrust them at
us, and retreated. Picking up their hoes, they explained from a safe
distance: 'We heard that you're on hunger strike for rights. And that
they keep you half-starved all the time, anyway. So we had a whip-
round – everything that's in those packets will do you good. Eat
it when your hunger strike's finished!'
    Returning to the house, we unwrap the parcels. Carrots, white
bread, a couple of cubes of butter . . . a whole packet of sugar! Who
were these women who gathered such gifts for us, bit by bit? What
motivated them – they, who barely knew anything about the 'rights'
for which we struggled – to support us despite the risk of being
caught? And in the light of their action, what price the theories aired
by some that our people are unaware of their oppressed situation
and feel no need for civil liberties? When I was much younger and
thought myself unique in my wisdom, I, too, was guilty of such an
attitude towards those who grew the bread I ate or sewed summer
dresses (little did I know that just such dresses are sewn in the
camps). At that time I yearned to emigrate, 'to get out of this swamp'.
Now, finding myself an émigrée by force of circumstances, I have
come to understand that, which I did not comprehend then.
    Thank you, O Lord, that it fell to my lot to endure the rigours of
prison transports, to hide poetry and books from the KGB, to languish
in punishment cells and to starve. Only when I entered into open
combat did I realise how much help I received from almost everyone
I encountered.

Irina Ratushinskaya, from *Grey is the colour of hope*

207   Revolution is . . .

revolution is . . .
>   when the first ray of light
>   slashes night and day asunder

revolution is . . .
>   when a woman gives birth
>   with her thumb raised high
>   urging 'Amandla!'

revolution is . . .
>   when a child marches from a womb
>   with a raised clenched fist
>   saying 'mama we are on our own!'

revolution is . . .
>   when consciousness tear the mask
>   hiding my sister's beautiful face
>   redeeming her blackness

revolution is . . .
>   when pick-axes and ploughs
>   pause to determine the worth
>   of sweat on labouring backs

revolution is . . .
>   when a forest rises to sharpen
>   its branches like pencils
>   then poetry will inscribe
>   the song of the river in ink

Essop Patel

208   Down in a slum a new born babe
stirs in her sleep.
She wakes, she looks,
she looks into my eyes.
She looks into my eyes
and I know we have hope;
I hope we have hope.

An Indian woman

209 The Ministry of children

Lord, your word has been presented to us by our children.
It has come to us through their words, their expressive gestures
and their manner of interpreting the gospel and the facts of life.
Little children are often considered
as beings that must only receive
and submit themselves to the power of big grown-ups.
People think they can give something
only on the sentimental level.
Instead, in bearing witness to life,
in the deeds, the expressions
and the drive towards high ideals of children and teenagers
we have to discover human values
indispensible for the path of history.
Moreover, the christian community must discover here the
authentic proclamation of your word;
it must accept this human dialogue
which involves faith and life and calls for clear cut choices.
From now on we will try to consider children
as people capable of giving a notable contribution to society
and we want to give them room
in the community and in the neighbourhood.
This engagement is called for
because of important social reasons and,
for us, it also is evangelically inspired.
In fact, Jesus, thought very highly of children.
He considered them an essential component
of that world of the 'least' and 'the little ones'
upon which society, history and the Kingdom of God rest.
He made himself little
and fully subjected himself to poverty and partook in the
destiny of the masses at the bottom of society.

Isolotto Community, Latin America, written with the help of children

210   A child from the dark depressing ghetto land of Belfast had a great week at Corrymeela. On her departure as she was about to board the minibus for Belfast, she looked out to sea and said 'Goodbye sea'. Then looking up to the clear blue sky she said 'Goodbye sky'. Lastly she looked at her new friends, helpers and leaders, with whom she had played and worshipped, to them she said 'Goodbye God'. She then climbed into the bus for her journey back to her closed ghetto community.

Corrymeela Link

211   If we will let them, children will lead us to the freedom that is their heritage. To creative day-dreaming, to wonder over truth, and into Narnia' we seek.

     They will teach us something about limits and littleness, tenderness and transparency. And something about the upside-down kingdom where paupers become princes and cripples dance and Zaccheus has the best view. If we will be like them, we may yet grope our way back into an enduring hope and a sense of adventure, elements for which we were designed.

Joan Puls, from *Every Bush is Burning*

212   Batter my heart, three-person'd God, for you
As yet but knock, breathe, shine, and seek to mend,
That I may rise and stand, o'erthrow me, and bend
Your force to break, blow, burn, and make me new.
I, like an usurp'd town, to another due
Labour to admit you, but O, to no end!
Reason, your viceroy in me, me should defend,
But is captiv'd and proves weak or untrue.

Yet dearly I love you, and would be loved fain,
But am betrothed unto your enemy:
Divorce me, untie, or break that knot again
Take me to you, imprison me, for I
Except you enthral me, never shall be free,
Nor ever chaste, except you ravish me.

John Donne

213   One thing stirs me when I look back at my youthful days, it is the fact that so many people gave me something or were something to me without knowing it. Such people had a decisive influence on me; they entered into my life and became powers within me. Much that I should not otherwise have felt so clearly, or done so effectively, was felt or done as it was, because I stand, as it were, under the sway of these people. Hence I always think that we all live spiritually by what others have given us in the significant hours of life.

These significant hours do not announce themselves as coming, but arrive unexpectedly. Nor do they make a great show of themselves; they pass almost unperceived. Often, indeed, their significance comes home to us first, as we look back. Much that has become our own in gentleness, modesty, kindness, willingness to forgive, in veracity, loyalty, resignation under suffering, we owe to people in whom we have seen or experienced these virtues at work, sometimes in a great matter, sometimes in a small. A thought which had become act sprang into us like a spark, and lighted a new flame within us.

If we had before us those who have thus been a blessing to us, and could tell them how it came about, they would be amazed to learn what passed over from their life into ours.

Albert Schweitzer, from *Memories of Childhood and Youth*

214   Leaders are best
When people barely know that they exist
Not so good when people obey and acclaim them
Worst when they despise them.
But of a good leader who talks little,
When their work is done
Their aim fulfilled
They will say 'We did it ourselves'.

Lao Tzu

215 Coming in silence

'We were friends who understood each other totally.' Rostropovich says of the 'deep and introverted' composer. The nature of that friendship can be heard not just in the words spoken by Rostropovich's interpreter during our interview, but in the cellist's tone of voice in Russian and in his excursions into eccentrically broken but unusually expressive English.

He gives an example of their friendship. In the 1950s there were times when, late at night, there would be telephone calls from Shostakovich. 'Slava, Slava,' the composer would plead, using Rostropovich's familiar name, 'immediately, you have to come see me. Immediately, I need you to come.'

'I think to myself,' says Rostropovich, 'maybe he wants to speak about some concert coming up — because at that time we went on some small tours together. He would play the piano, and I the cello in performance of his music. So I would go to him. And he would move a chair over to his desk, just the way we are sitting now, and say, "Sit, Slava, sit." '

Rostropovich leans forward, imitating the composer's welcoming gesture, combining need and conspiratorial friendship. 'And then he would say, "Slava, now let's just be quiet." '

Slava sits before me for a moment, the pause lending emphasis to the point. 'And we'd sit there not looking at each other. It was like an eternity. First of all, I was still young. Can you imagine? To go without a single word for the span of 15 minutes? And then he would get up and say. "Thank you, thank you, Slava, for coming to see me." And I would go.'

Why the silence? 'He just needed human warmth. Somebody who would radiate warmth, who would understand everything that was happening to him without explanation. So he wouldn't need words, wouldn't need to say anything. That's the way I explain it. And I would leave and also have a feeling of relief. Somehow we relieved each other.'

Edward Rothstein, from *The Independent Sunday Magazine*

216 A good man

'No son could have done more for his mother – and especially when – never mind. I just thought I'd tell you. Edwin's a good man.'

She left him and he went into the kitchen for his tea thinking 'a good man, a good man'. When she had said it of Edwin, he had wished that it could be said of him. The words had pricked his childhood landscape, when to be good was the best you could be. And even though his idea of a good man had been diluted and twisted – now it was the man who achieved himself in whatever fashion, now it was said of someone who did a good turn, now of someone who avoided the vulgar or obvious, mostly it was said as a sarcastic dig – yet when, as then, it was clearly said, it drew on more of him, resounded more lingeringly in his mind than any other phrase. The world became ordered once more, a simple moral form, an acceptable hierarchy, and yet without the fear that must attend a hierarchy of power, or the deceit which always attends a hierarchy of birth or the injustice which attends a hierarchy of money or merit – with warmth only, and the dignity which came from the assumption that in any circumstances a man can act well – and that is enough.

But why the need for a hierarchy? Service, Patriotism, Heroism, Honour, Duty – all the big hierarchical words which had once stirred him, he had seen peeled of their capitals. Ambition, Magnificence, Greatness, which had raised columns to other piles of hierarchy, they, too, were tattered. Many words had gone – and many he still wished good riddance to – all except 'Goodness'. And if what it evoked in him was to do with the past rather than the present, with retrogression rather than progress, with evasion rather than confrontation, then he was prepared to accept these accusations. For that one word alone, its meaning and its history, stood intact among the debris, and if a man's life lay in becoming – as Richard believed – in aspiring, in moving towards, then some gradation and so hierarchy was needed to give that movement legitimacy. 'A good man': to be that would be something.

Melvyn Bragg, from *Without a city wall*

217 Nurse on duty

Rising into the city sky
The clock tower chimes its quarter hours
Above a world where man is served
By man, each new day;
And starting early or ending late.
Work is never sleeping here.

Walking with us as we watch
The vital level of the mercury,
And feed into the hungry veins
The steady saline drips,
Inject the kind release of pain,
And soothe the hearts of those ashamed to cry,
And chase the busy round of linen skips,
There is a God who cares;
Through the unexpected and routine,
Emergency procedure and resuscitation team,
Even when the laboured breathing stops
And Death stands there
To greet the God who cares.

Down the long white ward I walk,
Among the youngest here, yet proud
To be a part –
And prouder still because I know
That in the quiet and the haste,
In both the squalor and the grace,
Behind the geriatric's toothless grins,
The spastic's ageworn lines of suffering,
Behind the grinding noise of sluice machine,
The hours of dressing wounds and keeping clean,
There is a God who cares.

Let these hands that fill the fluid charts
Be kind, as His were kind;
Let love shine in these eyes
As once in His they shone,
And may these feet run to seek thy will,
As day by day, from bed to bed I go;
And may I serve
With strength and joy
The God who cares.

Carey Jane Howell
written while working on her first ward at Queen Elizabeth Hospital, Birmingham.

218   The Stranger

Why were the Jews so angry with Jesus
that day when he preached
in the Synagogue at Nazareth
that they attempted to kill him?
Was it because he dared to say
he saw the movement of God
in the action of a poor widow
of another race?
It was not the righteous people of God
but the stranger,
from her experience of poverty and famine,
who shared her food.
And he saw God's presence
in the unbelieving Naaman
who came from Syria, another race,
and recognised the true prophet
and asked to be healed.
In Christ,
God himself broke into life,
coming in from outside,
a stranger.

The stranger is rarely welcome;
he sees too clearly
our empty respectable ways,
our narrow vision
and the chains of our religion.
He sides with outcasts
and offends good worthy church folk.
He is always present,
coming from the streets,
the Third World,
from prison,
naked and hungry
piercing our ignorance
with insights
and lessons
from his own bitter experience.

Author unknown

219   'I met a stranger yestere'en:
      I put food in the eating place;
      Drink in the drinking place
      Music in the listening place,
      And in the sacred name of the Triune,
      He blessed myself and my house,
      My cattle and my dear ones;
      And the lark sang in his song,
         often, often, often
      Comes the Christ in strangers' guise
         often, often, often
      Comes the Christ in strangers' guise.'

      An ancient Celtic rune

220   The Chief Rabbi of Lyons was a Jewish chaplain to the French forces
      in the 1914-1918 war. One day a wounded man staggered into a trench
      and told the Rabbi that a Roman Catholic was on the point of death
      in no-man's land, and was begging that his padre should come to
      him with a crucifix. The padre could not quickly be found. The Jew
      rapidly improvised a cross, ran out with it into no-man's land, and
      was seen to hold it before the dying man's eyes. He was almost
      immediately shot by a sniper; the bodies of the Catholic and the Jew
      were found together.

      Victor Gollancz

221   We who lived in concentration camps can remember the men who
      walked through the huts comforting others, giving away their last
      piece of bread. They may have been few in number, but they offer
      sufficient proof that everything can be taken from a man but one
      thing: the last of the human freedoms – to choose one's attitude
      in any given set of circumstances, to choose one's way.

      Viktor Frankl, from *Man's Search for Meaning*

222 The other half of a missionary

Now, never send a Missionary into a heathen country without his
wife. If you send a Missionary who is a single man, he is only half
a Missionary. When you send him with his wife, he is a whole
Missionary. *(Laughter and cheering)* We men look to the Missionaries
and respect them; but how are our females to be advanced, unless
you send Missionaries' wives? Now then, the Missionary is respected
by the men, and the Missionary's wife is respected by our females;
and that excellent woman, the Missionary's wife, teaches our females
not to be tramped down as we did tramp them down when we were
heathen. They teach them to be respected more. They say, 'Come
up, come up,' and they are up. *(Cheers)* Why, there was a time when
a poor woman could not say anything against her lord, for fear of
the tomahawk.

From a speech by the Rev. Peter Jacobs, Hudson's Bay, 1851

223 Two-way mission

The Church in India has been perceived to be a 'receiving' Church.
Our funds, theology, ideas, leaders and concepts of service all seem
to come to us often from the West. This has created dependency and
a sense of alienation from the rest of India. The time has come for
us to see how we can be a 'giving' community. We have talented and
educated people amongst our members. We have funds and other
resources that can be mobilised and we have our institutions and
experience that can be used by others. There is so much need around
us, in India and neighbouring countries. When will we realise that
we can share our experience and resources? Mission and partnership
must be a two-way process of love, trust and willingness to learn
and grow together.

Daleep S Mukarji

224 Yad Vashem

At Yad Vashem, Jerusalem, a large outdoor sculpture by
Nandor Glid commemorates Holocaust victims.

We did not find Him
In the Bazaar
On the Way of the Cross,
So we bought bright baubles
And carried carved camels.
Our ersatz experience
Cost thirty pieces.

Then we came to a place
Where skeletal forms
Stretched starkly under a livid sky.
Backs arched
In one continual agony
Over the twisted iron limbs;
Fingers spread like giant thorns
Pushing us away;
Skulls screamed silently,
Accusing us
Who were not there when it happened –
Or were we?

It was this –
This metal monument of death
Which pierced our apathy
And brought us back to life again.
We shed our tears then,
Burning with shame and grief.

And we found Him there –
Weeping with us.

Margaret Connor

225   **Beatitudes ... for friends of handicapped people**

Blessed are you who take time to listen to difficult speech,
    for you help us to know that if we
    persevere we can be understood.

Blessed are you who walk with us in public places and ignore
the stares of strangers
    for in your companionship we find havens
    of relaxation.

Blessed are you who never bid us to 'hurry up', and more
blessed you who do not snatch our tasks from us,
    for often we need time rather than help.

Blessed are you who stand beside us when we enter new and
untried adventures,
    for our failures will be outweighed by the
    times when we surprise ourselves and you.

Blessed are you who ask for our help,
    for our greatest need is to be needed.

Blessed are you who help us with the graciousness of Christ
who did not bruise the reed nor quench the flax,
    for often we need the help we cannot ask for.

Blessed are you when, by all these things,
you assure us that the thing that makes us
individuals is not in our peculiar muscles,
nor in our wounded nervous system, but in the
God-given self that no infirmity can confine.

Rejoice and be exceedingly glad, and know
that you give us reassurance that could never
be spoken in words, for you deal with us as
God has dealt with all his children.

Anon

226   Blessed are the poor
   not the penniless, but those whose heart is free.
Blessed are those who mourn
   not those who whimper, but those who raise their voices.
Blessed are those who hunger and thirst for justice
   not those who whine, but those who struggle.
Blessed are the merciful
   not those who forget, but those who forgive.
Blessed are the pure in heart
   not those who act like angels, but those whose life is
   transparent.
Blessed are the peace-makers
   not those who shun conflict, but those who face it
   squarely.
Blessed are those who are persecuted for justice
   not because they suffer, but because they love.

P. Jacob, *Santiago Chile*

227   **Pentecost is Every Day**

I share and share and share again
sometimes with a new language
which, if you are so open
will take you behind the sky
and award you cartwheels across the sun
I give and give and give again
not restricted by the church calendar
or concocted ritual
I have no need of anniversaries
for I have always been
I speak and speak and speak again
with the sting of purity
that can only be Me
causing joyous earthquakes in the mourning soul of man
I am and am and am again

Stewart Henderson

228 Pilgrimage

'Where are you going?'
  'From nowhere to somewhere.'
'How long will it take you?'
  'From now until then.'
'What will you find there?'
  'The past as a present.'
'How will you use it?'
  'I know not. Amen.'

'What are you packing?'
  'A suitcase of sleeping.'
'Why is it heavy?'
  'It bulges with night.'
'In what is its value?'
  'Goods one can trade with.'
'How will you bargain?'
  'I know not. Amen.'

'Who will go with you?'
  'A child and an old man.'
'How will they travel?'
  'On the backs of the dead.'
'What will they live on?'
  'Bread, wine and blessings.'
'Will they survive then?'
  'I trust so. Amen.'

'What will the land be?'
  'Sand, thorns and granite.'
'Why do you want it?'
  'As the garden I need.'
'How will you shape it?'
  'With songs keen as sickles.'
'When will it flower?'
  'From now until then.'

Nadine Brummer

Lamb of God

Lamb of God,
you take away the sins of the world:
have mercy on us.

Lamb of God

When prisoner 16670, held in a Nazi concentration camp, deliberately steps into a line of men condemned to death and takes the place of a man about to die (*item 232*), or when a surgeon, after a seven hour operation, is so drained that he has to be led away by the hand (*item 238*), we are witnessing human experiences that take us very close to Calvary. We glimpse the possibility that frail humanity might become a lamb of God, self-giving for the sake of others.

Most of us are further away than that but we echo Christopher von Wyk: 'My nose has never sniffed teargas but I weep all the same (*item 245*). The cross of Christ was much more than the silent sharing of tears (*item 247*) but to shed them in genuine solidarity with those whom life has shattered raises a corner of understanding about what the cross means.

229 The agony of God

I listen to the agony of God –
I who am fed,
who never yet went hungry for a day.
I see the dead –
the children starved for lack of bread –
I see and try to pray.

I listen to the agony of God –
I who am warm
who never yet lacked a sheltering home.
In dull alarm
the dispossessed of hut and farm
aimless and transient roam.

I listen to the agony of God –
I who am strong
with health and love and laughter in my soul.
I see a throng
of stunted children reared in wrong
and wish to make them whole.

I listen to the agony of God –
But know full well
That not until I share their bitter cry –
earth's pain and hell –
can God within my spirit dwell
to bring the Kingdom nigh.

I was hungry not just for food
    but for peace that comes from a pure heart.
I was thirsty not for water
    but for peace that satiates the passionate thirst for war.
I was naked not for clothes
    but for that beautiful dignity of men and
    women for their bodies.

I was homeless not for a shelter made of bricks
but for a heart that understands, that covers.
that loves.

I was hungry; I was thirsty; I was naked;
I was homeless.
    Yet I found peace, peace and dignity and
    a heart that loves.

Nancy Telfer

230 Jesus you were executed on a cross;
You had no army, no resources,
no connections with the elite.

My heart is trembling.
Couldn't you have declared yourself ruler of the earth?
Why didn't you establish the Kingdom?

Why these millions of bitter sighs?
Why these tears of angers, and
broken hopes?
Why that naked despair in the eyes
of the little boy – my boy –
as he tried to escape the machine guns?

It is as if you were not risen
as if the promise were not ours
as if we had to be afraid
as if your power were not present
in our weakness.

And yet, are we not sharing in your Cross?
Are we not with you in your rejection?
And are we not beginning to live in God's acceptance?
And can we not express your love through our pain?

Adapted from a South African poem

231 The Cross in the community of Madras should find its place in identification with our suffering people. The Church has been far from a suffering community. Our Christianity has been a comfortable Christianity. We need to be stripped like Christ was on the Cross and suffer with our people. We need a greater and keener sense of identification with the Cross . . . We need to get back to the grassroots. We need to get back to the average men in the village. We need to know humanity as it really exists in the majority of our people. Human existence in India is a suffering existence. It is in reality a reliving of the Cross . . . Over 60% of our people are starving, undernourished, ill-provided, suppressed, oppressed and discriminated against.

Let us seek to identify ourselves with the suffering of our people. That would make Lent more meaningful. Let us hunger a little more with the hungry. Let us thirst a little more with the thirsty. Let us seek to know the oppression and the oppressed, the injustices and hardships of our brothers and sisters. In this light the Cross will be more meaningful to us . . .

Sundar Clarke, India

232 At seven p.m. the camp's deputy commandant Karl Fritzsch appeared, accompanied by Gestapo chief Gerhardt Palitzsch. Two archetypal, jack-booted Nazi supermen: Fritzsch had personally supervised the first mass murder of prisoners by means of the Cyclon B gas which had originally been manufactured for the extermination of vermin; while Palitzsch, a torturer of some renown, proudly boasted that he had executed 2,500 prisoners with his own hands.

Slowly, wordlessly, they passed down the lines, their elegant uniforms contrasting starkly with the scarecrow rags of the men. Fritzsch pointed a finger, an SS man pushed a hapless man out of line, Palitzsch noted the man's number in his book, while another SS man began to form a new line of victims.

Seven . . . eight . . . nine. As the ninth man was selected, he uttered an agonised cry: 'My wife, my children, I shall never see them again.' His choking sobs pierced the silence, while the scarecrows looked at him unmoved. For them the ordeal was almost over. Nine down, only one to go. They held their breath.

For what happened in the next few minutes we have the sworn testimony of several witnesses, and their accounts are remarkably consistent. Suddenly a small, slight figure detached itself from the ranks, walked briskly towards the group of SS men and stood to attention before Fritzsch. The man removed his regulation cap as he did so. It was number 16670 – a prisoner whose cheeks had an unhealthy flush and who wore round spectacles in wire frames.

Something like animation stirred at last among the men. This was unheard of. That anyone should dare to step out of line during an Appel was unthinkable. Surely the crazy fool would be kicked senseless or shot out of hand by the Gestapo. They watched and waited.

The moment passed. The crazy fool remained alive. Perhaps Fritzsch's sheer astonishment inhibited his usual responses. 16670 pointed to the distraught man who had cried out, and asked, very calmly, in correct German, if he might take his place. The prisoners gasped. Perhaps Fritzsch gasped too, for he asked in amazement: 'Who are you?' (He did not normally enter into conversation with sub-humans.) 'A Catholic priest,' came the reply, as though that was all that needed to be said.

Incredulously, and indeed incredibly, Fritzsch nodded assent, gestured to the reprieved man, one Franciszek Gajowniczek, to return to his place in the line. Palitzsch replaced one number by another, ordered the condemned men to remove their shoes, and sent them off, to be stripped of their rags and buried alive. Next to the last in line went Raymund Kolbe, Father Maximilian, number 16670. As he was flung naked onto the concrete floor of that grisly cell, did he recall that centuries ago St. Francis had asked one of his friars to lay him naked on the bare earth to die?

Mary Craig, from *Candles in the dark*

233   The Sin of the world touches us, each one.
We cannot escape it.
We share its shame,
  its ill-gotten gains,
  its guilt.

The Sin of the world is my sins,
I am sorry, Lord;
sorry to the point where sorrow hurts,
sorry to the depths of my life,
sorry to the place where renewal is my only hope,
I am truly sorry, Lord

Lamb of God, you take away the Sin of the world;
have mercy on us.

Donald Hilton

234 Stripped to the bone

I tear my hungry baby from my breast
To come and care for yours.
Yours grows up fine,
But, oh God, not mine!
From beach and school yours I fetch
And wonder if school mine did reach.

Your man comes home at night
A welcome and delight,
Wineglass in hand,
Red chair in front of fire bright.
To bed you go and make love.

My bed is empty and cold
For all my energy is drained away,
My man and I too soon feel old,
Can you still look me in the eye
And ask me what is wrong
After you've stripped me to the bone?

You win and take everything I own
And still you want my home,
What have I done that you won't leave me alone.

Gladys Thomas, South Africa

235   Elizabeth Pilenko came from a wealthy land-owning family in the south of Russia. She became a keen socialist revolutionary and during the years 1914-17 her life was taken up with revolutionary activities. After the October Revolution she worked with extraordinary skill and audacity in rescuing victims from the Terror. In 1923 she came to Paris. She found her way back to religious faith. She presented herself to the authorities of the Russian Church in Paris and announced that she wished to become a religious, 'Beginning at once, today,' and to found a monastery. She had her way, but she was not the traditional Russian Orthodox religious. She was accused by some of neglecting the long services and the traditional contemplation. 'I must go my way,' she said, 'I am for the suffering people.'

When the German occupation took place Mother Maria summoned her chaplain and told him that she felt that her particular duty was to render all possible assistance to persecuted Jews. She knew that this would mean imprisonment and probable death, and she gave him the option of leaving. He refused. For a month the convent was a haven for Jews. Women and children were hidden within its walls. Money poured in to enable them to escape from France and hundreds got away. At the end of the month the Gestapo came. Mother Maria was arrested and sent to the concentration camp at Ravensbrueck. Her chaplain was sent to Buchenwald, where he died of starvation and overwork.

She was known even to the guards as 'that wonderful Russian nun,' and it is doubtful whether they had any intention of killing her. She had been there two and a half years when a new block of buildings was erected in the camp, and the prisoners were told that these were to be hot baths. A day came when a few dozen prisoners from the women's quarters were lined up outside the buildings. One girl became hysterical. Mother Maria, who had not been selected, came up to her, 'Don't be frightened,' she said, 'look, I shall take your turn,' and in line with the rest, she passed through the doors. It was Good Friday, 1945.

From *the Christian News-Letter*

236 A Prayer for Empathy

Loving Heavenly Father –

You know us
through and through
and love us just the same.
Give us your awareness
of others
and by your Holy Spirit
make us sensitive
to them.

Let us hurt
where they hurt,
even to weep with them,
that they may know
they are not alone.

Let us enter
into their joys,
to laugh and rejoice
with them
at those things
which set them free.

Work through
our imaginations
enabling us to offer
quietly
needful help,
encouragement
or a word in season.

All this we ask
for the sake
of Your Son our Saviour
Jesus Christ.
                    Amen

Susan Appleby

237   **Engine room**

Into this quiet room
the stories come,
a centrifugal coil.
Her pain, his toil,
frantic mother, errant brother,
coming baby, prisoned father,
anxious daughter – still they gather,
hurled
from a hurt world,
drawn in
to where we spin.

Into this quiet room
the stories come,
end-split fibres, rough
textured stuff,
grist to the mills of God.
Our spindle turns a mill,
dare not be still.
Tighten the slack, pull the ends in,
painfully spin
his fears, her tears,
this one's sorrow, their tomorrow,
someone's past – all pass
through this wheel
into the mill.

Out of this quiet place
the spun prayers race,
a centripetal fan
of firm spun yarn.
So grind the mills of God.
Within this quiet room
we twist a strand
may ease the human loom,
dovetail the weaving,
somehow, at secondhand,
lessen the grieving.

Anne Ashworth

238 Self giving

A doctor tells of an operation which, as a young student, he observed in a London hospital. It was an operation of the greatest delicacy, in which a small error would have had fatal consequences. In the outcome the operation was a triumph: but it involved seven hours of intense and uninterrupted concentration on the part of the surgeon. When it was over, a nurse had to take him by the hand, and lead him from the operating theatre like a blind man or a little child. This, one might say, is what self-giving is like: such is the likeness of God, wholly given, spent and drained in that sublime self-giving which is the ground and source and origin of the universe.

W.H. Vanstone, from *Love's Endeavour Love's Expense*

239 Lord, when I am hungry, give me someone in need of food:
when I am thirsty, send me someone needing a drink;
when I am cold, send me someone to warm;
when I am grieved, offer me someone to console;
when my cross grows heavy, let me share another's cross;
when I am poor, lead me to someone in need;
when I have no time, give me someone I can help a little while;
when I am humiliated, let me have someone to praise;
when I am disheartened, send me someone to cheer;
when I need understanding, give me someone who needs mine;
when I need to be looked after, send me someone to care for;
when I think only of myself, draw my thoughts to another . . .

Co-workers of Mother Teresa in Japan

240 My earliest recollection of Mother Teresa is her attending to lepers in the slums of Howrah – a Calcutta suburb. If Calcutta is wretched Howrah is even more so, more uncared for, more potholed, more sunk in its garbage, more crowded, more pestilential, a heavily industrialised area overwhelmed by pollution and unemployment.

Some eighty lepers had gathered themselves in an abysmal cul de sac. The huts were visibly decayed, the open drains were choked with human waste, and the whole place stank.

As we approached the lepers, huddled, grey, and limbless, we passed a boy defaecating in the drain. It seemed his guts were pouring out. When I drew Mother's attention to him, she gave him a look as stoical as his own, and observed that he was suffering from an advanced case of dysentery, and that she would attend to him later. This, remember, was the first time I had met Mother, so I might be forgiven for mentally accusing her of indifference. It was only later I came to appreciate that she was there to attend lepers – and that but for a single helper, a slight young girl in a white sari, she was alone and inadequately equipped. But she did tell her helper to get the boy's name and address so that they could treat him later.

I had gone to write an article and take photographs, expecting to see yet another of those dedicated white women doing their bit for the poor of India, women genuinely moved by the plight of others and with the will to do something despite their many other commitments and ties. Here I was confronted by a foreigner, not in a suitable dress or uniform that would somehow make her efforts understandable, but by a woman in humble, blue-bordered, white sari. Here again, I had my reservations. Having been born and brought up in India I never fail to feel uncomfortable, and very wary, of foreigners who find it necessary to wear Indian dress to establish their sense of belonging. But here was a perfectly ordinary woman in a perfectly ordinary sari, completely innocent of affectations, who I felt instinctively was no passing phenomenon. She had the feeling of permanence, of a person who was going to continue working the way she was that day for as long as she lived. I was yet to know that she had severed all ties; that she had dedicated herself to the service of the poor.

Desmond Doigs, from *Mother Teresa; her people and her work*

241   Every time I give a piece of bread, I give it to Him. That is why we must find the hungry and the naked. That is why we are totally bound to the poor. The poor must know that we love them, that they are wanted. They themselves have nothing to give but love. We are concerned how to get this message of love and compassion across. We are trying to bring peace to the world through our work.

Mother Teresa

242   **Proving faith**

I cannot pass my faith on to others
   as a doctor injects a patient with serum.
I cannot pass my faith on to others
   as a service-station attendant fills a car with petrol.
I cannot pass my faith on to others
   as wharf-labourers move cargo from one ship to another
   with cranes.
I cannot provide a pill that produces faith when it is swallowed.
I cannot explain my faith as a teacher explains a mathematical
   formula.
I cannot demonstrate my faith as a clever lawyer demonstrates
   the innocence of the accused to a sceptical judge.
I can only prove my faith by letting Christ heal my entangled,
   sinful life.
I can only prove my faith by praying for others, as Christ prayed
   for Peter and others.
I can only prove my faith by doing loving deeds to others, even
   as Christ revealed his love to the sick and hungry.
I can only prove my faith by being ready to forgive and forget
   the evil words and deeds of others, even as Christ forgave
   His enemies on the cross.
I can only prove my faith by being prepared to suffer for others,
   even as Christ suffered for others.
I can only prove my faith by not letting my failures deflect me
   from my calling, even as Christ could not be deflected from
   His course by the people's unbelief.
I can only prove my faith through the power of the Holy Spirit,
   given by Christ.

John Gnanabaranam

243 **Flowers are not enough**

I have no words to meet your pain –
and words and flowers are not enough;
each time I come your life has shrunk
from room to chair, and now your bed;
my comfort sounds a platitude
too trite it's better left unsaid.

Silence drops minutes drip on drip –
and all I have is love to give.
I grope in darkness for a prayer,
and sooth your brow and watch each tear;
I feel a pauper in your need –
it's not enough that I am here.

Cecily Taylor

244 **A child's burden**

My mother's name is worry,
In summer, she worries about water;
In winter, she worries about coal briquets,
and all year long she worries about rice.

In day time, my mother worries about living;
At night, she worries for her children,
and all the day long she worries and worries.

Then, my mother's name is worry.
My father's name is drunken frenzy.
And mine is tear and sigh.

A Korean schoolgirl, 12 years

245   Me, I cry easily if you're hurt
      and I would've carried the crosses
      of both the murderer
      and the thief
      if they'd've let me
      and I'd've lived then.

      I grasp helplessly at cigarettes
      during riots
      and burn my fingers hoping.

      My nose has never sniffed teargas
      but I weep all the same
      and my heart hurts
      aching from buckshot.

      My dreams these days are policed
      by a million eyes
      that baton-charge my sleep
      and frog-march me into a
      shaken morning.

      I can't get used to injustice.
      I can't smile no matter what.

      I'll never get used to nightmares
      but I often dream of freedom.

      Christopher van Wyk

246 Tears

Thank God for tears,
the tears that flow unchecked,
that run in rivulets
down to the sea of God;
that have to merge eventually
with something larger than the self.

Thank God for tears,
the tears that bring release
for knotted nerves
twisted as sinews,
bringing a breathing out
beyond despair.

Thank God for tears,
and then beyond the tears,
beyond the hopelessness
that has to offer up the grief
till no more fall,
because no more can fall –

the tiny step that is a journey's start,
a slow step onward,
numb at first and seeming dead,
where haltingly, but gradually
one grassblade starts to grow
watered by tears;
somehow a kind of healing can begin.

Cecily Taylor

247   A colleague has recently described to me an occasion when a West Indian woman in a London flat was told of her husband's death in a street accident. The shock of grief stunned her like a blow, she sank into a corner of the sofa and sat there rigid and unhearing. For a long time her terrible tranced look continued to embarrass the family, friends and officials who came and went. Then the school teacher of one of her children, an Englishwoman, called and, seeing how things were, went and sat beside her. Without a word she threw an arm around the tight shoulders, clasping them with her full strength. The white cheek was thrust hard against the brown. Then as the unrelenting pain seeped through to her the newcomer's tears began to flow, falling on their two hands linked in the woman's lap. For a long time that is all that was happening. And then at last the West Indian woman started to sob. Still not a word was spoken and after a little while the visitor got up and went, leaving her contribution to help the family meet its immediate needs. That is the embrace of God, his kiss of life.

John V. Taylor, from *The Go-Between God*.

248   Where can I go?

If there is not a place where tears are understood,
Where can I go to cry?
If there is not a place where my spirit can take wing,
Where do I go to fly?
If there is not a place where my questions can be asked,
Where do I go to seek?
If there is not a place where my feelings can be heard,
Where do I go to speak?
If there is not a place where I can try and learn and grow,
Where can I just be me?

Author unknown, from *Compass News*

249 Tired
And lonely,
So tired
The heart aches,
Meltwater trickles
Down the rocks,
The fingers are numb,
The knees tremble.
It is now,
Now, that you must not give in.

On the path of the others
Are resting places,
Places in the sun
Where they can meet.
But this
Is your path,
And it is now,
Now, that you must not fail.

Weep
If you can,
Weep,
But do not complain
The way chose you –
And you must be thankful.

Dag Hammarskjöld

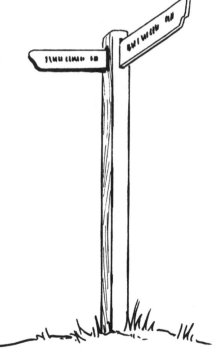

Grant us peace

Lamb of God,
you take away the sins of the world
grant us peace

Grant us peace

'Peace is not a thing to possess, but a way of possessing' (*item 257*). Peace is more than the absence of war, though, as we 'Remember Ypres, the Somme, Mons and Verdun' (*item 251*) the invitation to peace is heard more powerfully.

One of the insights of recent times lies in the recognition that peace cannot be considered in isolation. The 'Justice, Peace, and the Integrity of Creation' process is a reminder of the wholeness of life and the inter-relatedness of all created things. The call to peace involves hearing the children ask, 'What kind of a world is this that the adult people are going to leave for us children?' (*item 261*). Such conviction will dedicate lavatories (*item 267*), ask questions about pollution and the use of resources, and learn to say 'we' rather than 'I' (*item 279*).

Remembering...

250 November wind
leaves the year's end
shredded to rags,
pruned branches
for bonfires.
Coloured stars
against the night's back-drop
mere illusions of merriment.

The usual mist
a pall
to drape the Cenotaph
and a thousand village greens
stained with blood-red poppies.

Those old enough
for torn memories
stop the year,
stand grey-haired
to the autumn chill;

for those who are too young
gratitude hangs
like tattered regimental flags
in a cathedral.

Some hearts still ache –
lives pocked with craters
where love might have been –
blitzed promises and unborn hopes.

It is freedom we reap;
the price rocketed.
Concrete and glass have grafted
obvious scars,
but somewhere
in distant farmlands
ploughed into battlefields
acre upon acre –
the harvest of white crosses.

Cecily Taylor

251 Remember Ypres, the Somme, Mons and Verdun.
Remember the Western Desert, El Alamein, the Normandy beaches.
Remember Dresden, Hiroshima and the Burma Road.
Remember Korea, the Falkland Islands and Northern Ireland.

Remember the courage, the comradeship, the ingenuity,
the spirit of working together for a common cause,
the planning together for a better world
that would come with peace.

Remember the call to arms, the patriotic songs, the posters,
the partings which were such sweet sorrow,
the sound of the drum, the skirl of the pipe,
the prayer that God would be on our side.

Remember the carnage;
the colossal, stinking, bloody horror;
the ripped bodies on the wire,
the platoons of which only three out of forty lived.
Remember the widows of sixty years and more,
the old men and women living now who never knew their fathers.
Remember the love that was lost, the wisdom wasted,
the minds that were twisted and the limbs distorted.

Remember the wealth of nations being fired from guns,
dropped as bombs:
smashing schools, homes, factories, churches and hospitals;
ruining crops, destroying trees.
Remember the hope of a whole generation
left to evaporate in the sands of a desert
or sink forever in the oceans of the world.

Remember this day the children who will die while the world
spends its wealth on arms; the young who have no work while
others in their generation are trained to fight; the ambulances
that will not come while we argue about how many troop
carriers we need; the research into disease left neglected while
brilliant minds are used to study more effective destruction.

Remember the one who asked us to remember him.

Graham Cook

252 So Abram rose, and clave the wood, and went,
And took the fire with him, and a knife.
And as they sojourned both of them together,
Isaac the first-born spake and said, 'My Father,
Behold the preparations, fire and iron,
But where the lamb for this burnt-offering?'
Then Abram bound the youth with belts and straps,
And builded parapets and trenches there,
And stretchèd forth the knife to slay his son.
When lo! an angel called him out of heaven,
Saying, 'Lay not thy hand upon the lad,
Neither do anything to him. Behold,
A ram, caught in a thicket by its horns;
Offer the Ram of Pride instead of him.'
But the old man would not do so, but slew his son,
And half the seed of Europe, one by one.

Wilfred Owen

253 War ceased.
From Berlin's hill
Man cried, 'Be still.'

Be still?
When Europe's sons
Face worse than guns,
When men of might who fought for war
Still fight for Peace.

For Peace?
Man's heart shall know no peace
Until . . .

Until from Zion's hill
God cries, 'Be Still!'

Joyce Softley

254 Today

Today
There are people in the world
Who can boast
That today
Fourteen thousand people died.

Today
There are people
Who can talk about life after nuclear war
And not go mad.

Today
There are people who cry
And can see no solution.

Today
Are there people
Whose lives can change the way we live
Before life is destroyed?

Alison Head

255 Let Me Pass the Day in Peace

O God, you have let me pass the day in peace,
Let me pass the night in peace,
O Lord, you have no Lord.
There is no strength but in you.
There is no unity but in your house.
Under your hand I pass the night.
You are my mother and my father.
You are my home. Amen.

From *The Boran of Kenya*

Peace and Justice . . .

256 The Weight of a Snowflake

'Tell me the weight of a snowflake,' a coalmouse asked a wild dove.
'Nothing more than nothing,' was the answer.
'In that case, I must tell you a marvellous story,' the coalmouse said.
'I sat on the branch of a fir, close to its trunk, when it began to snow
– not heavily, not in a raging blizzard: no, just like in a dream,
without a sound and without any violence. Since I did not have
anything better to do, I counted the snowflakes settling on the twigs
and needles of my branch. Their number was exactly 3,741,952. When
the 3,741,953rd dropped onto the branch – nothing more than
nothing, as you say – the branch broke off'.

Having said that, the coalmouse flew away.

The dove, since Noah's time an authority on the matter, thought about
the story for while, and finally said to herself: 'Perhaps there is only
one person's voice lacking for peace to come to the world.'

Kurt Kauter, from *New Fables, Thus spoke the Marabou*

257 Peace is not a thing to possess, but a way of possessing:
Peace is not a gift to be given, but a way of giving:
Peace is not a topic to teach, but a way of teaching:
Peace is not a theory to learn, but a way of learning:
Peace is not an opinion to hold, but a way of holding:
Peace is not a resolution of strife, but a way of striving:
Peace is not a creed to preach, but a way of preaching:
Peace is not a God to serve, but a way of serving:
Peace is not a question to ask, but a way of asking:
Peace is not an answer to seek, but a way of seeking:
Peace is not a journey's end, but a way of journeying:

Richard Skinner

258 The Church must make clear choices. How can we see the pain, the suffering, the blood, the cruelty, and not make a choice for justice, peace and human freedom? If that choice means that we must openly oppose those who try to protect oppression and injustice through the use of gospel words like 'peace', 'reconciliation' and 'unity', then so be it.

Not that the unity of the church is not a legitimate concern. But we are also concerned with the truth without which the Church cannot live. We are concerned not so much about the common mind in the Church as about the faithful obedience of the Lord of the Church. If the unity of the church is not built upon the passion for truth, the desire for justice, the faithful obedience to the Lord whatever the cost, then it is not unity.

Allan Boesak, from *Walking on Thorns*

259 Christian society in Britain has domesticated the Gospel. It is geared to loving God in moderation. We may give alms to the poor, visit the sick and the lonely, hold annual bazaars and flag days for those in need – in fact do any good works which do not threaten the pattern of our society. But to demand justice at the expense of people's comfort or security – that makes us troublemakers.

Sheila Cassidy

260 Mother

If tomorrow, my mother,
Death should find me doubled over in a trench,
Don't weep.
The honour of your womb
Would then be my dead body.
My blood, the seed of new beginnings.
My life would then be a shout,
A flag symbolizing the struggle.

If tomorrow the enemy
Should place in your hands
My massacred body,
Don't weep.

Rather, be proud
That you gave our country
A son who would not be a slave,
Who preferred the silence
Of the centuries
To a moan produced
By the oppressor's lash.

Author unknown
This poem *Madre* was found stencilled on a wall in Leon, Nicaragua in 1979

261 What kind of a world?

God, what kind of world is this
that the adult people
are going to leave for us children?
There is fighting everywhere
and they tell us we live in a time of peace.
You are the only one who can help us.
Lord, give us a new world
in which we can be happy
in which we can have friends
and work together for a good future.
A world in which there will not be
any cruel people
who seek to destroy us and our world
in so many ways. Amen.

From *Children in Conversation with God, Lutheran World Federation*

262   I'm a peace-loving man,
but who is to say
if my children were starving for bread
that I wouldn't be violent?

I'm a peace-loving man,
but who is to say
that if somebody murdered my wife
I might not preach love any more?

You can keep all your talk –
your preaching as well,
I know if I lived in a similar hell
I'd be likely to act as they do.

I'm a peace-loving man;
O God, it is hard to find truth.
If it came to the crunch –
how would my theories stand then?

Cecily Taylor

263   If you come at me with your fists doubled,
    I think I can promise you
that mine will double as fast as yours;
    but if you come to me and say,
'Let us sit down and take counsel together,
    and, if we differ from one another,
understand just what the points at issue are,'
    we will presently find that we are not
so far apart after all,
    that the points on which we differ are few
and the points on which we agree are many.

Woodrow Wilson

264 Cost of living

Ever since I was born
Everyone's been complaining
how the cost of living
just keeps soaring:
    Tea from Ceylon
    Rice from Burma
    Sugar from Jamaica
Meat from the Argentine
Yes, there's no denying
the cost of living
has been rising
ever since I was born.

Yet I haven't heard
a single complaint
since the day I arrived
how the price of human lives
has been taking a nose-dive:
    in Hiroshima,
    Stalin's Russia,
    Hitler's Reich
in Vietnam,
    Kampuchea,
    Uganda,
    South Africa,
    Guatemala,
    El Salvador . . .

Ever since I was born
the cost of living
has been getting rather steep.
The cost of a life
has never been cheaper.

Cecil Rajendra

265   The terrible truth

Not even you Jesus
with your irresistible look
of infinite goodness
succeded in moving
the heart
of the rich young man
And yet, he, from his childhood
had kept
all the commandments.
Lord, my Lord, may we never
out of mistaken charity
water down
the terrible truths
you have spoken to the rich.

Helder Camara, from *A Thousand Reasons for Living*

266   Pie in the sky

We have been offered
   pie in the sky
but never smelled it,
neither will it appease
our hunger for rights
that are rightfully ours.

We watch through the window
   as you sit feasting
at a table loaded with equality
and grow frantic at its flavour.
How long can we retain
the rumble of hunger in our belly?

James Matthews

267 Dedication of a lavatory

In our new Colombia, Jesus, 200,000 people live on miserable settlements, with no drinking water. Six thousand families live piled together in the Majaguas terraces. There is one toilet for every four families. Dona Flor found out that their biggest problem is having to look after the girls when they go to the toilet, because if they go alone the caretakers take advantage of it and assault them.

Visiting a lavatory is not an act of 'good taste'. Writing about the experience is worse – and mentioning it to readers can cause offence. But a large part of this ministry can be found there, Jesus. We live in the filth, we breathe it until our lungs are saturated. To be poor means to live in squalor. As you will see, we have learned to read the Bible with these people from their point of view. And so we have discovered that their lives are the framework for our own Bible study.

I am convinced that if you take notice of them it is because they no longer have anyone on whom they can depend or to whom they can go for help. It is by breathing in the Spirit that their conscience is made clean. You are the one who keeps their rebellious instinct in check. Mind you, Jesus, they do suffer and they only rebel when they can't take any more. The poor are a generous and noble people. That is why, when they asked me to dedicate a lavatory, I went and dedicated it with all solemnity. That lavatory is a guarantee that from now on fewer children will die of worms in that neighbourhood. You, who loved the children so much, inspire me to do this work.

And so we press on and we'll meet on the way, Lord.

Juan Marcos Rivera, from *A letter to Jesus*

268 A religion true to its nature must also be concerned about man's social conditions. Religion deals with both earth and heaven, both time and eternity. Religion operates not only on the vertical plane but also on the horizontal. It seeks not only to integrate men with God but to integrate men with men and each man with himself. This means, at bottom, that the Christian gospel is a two-way road. On the one hand, it seeks to change the souls of men and thereby unite them with God; on the other hand, it seeks to change the environmental conditions of men so that the soul will have a chance after it is changed. Any religion that professes to be concerned with the souls of men and is not concerned with the slums that damn them, the economic conditions that strangle them, and the social conditions that cripple them is a dry-as-dust religion. Such a religion is the kind the Marxists like to see – an opiate of the people.

Martin Luther King

269 Christ among the Poor

Here am I,
where underneath the bridges
  in our winter cities
    homeless people sleep.
Here am I,
where in decaying houses
  little children shiver,
    crying at the cold.
Where are you?

Here am I,
with people in the line up,
  anxious for a hand-out,
    aching for a job.
Here am I,
when pensioners and strikers
  sing and march together,
    wanting something new.
Where are you?

Here am I,
where two or three are gathered,
  ready to be altered
    by the wine and bread.
Here am I,
when any new Zacchaeus
  gives away possessions,
    finds the way to life.
Where are you?

Where am I,
when priests and people wonder
  why the veil is broken
    at the holy place?
I have gone
where waifs and widows suffer:
  at the next Golgotha,
    loving to the end,
    Where are you?

Brian Wren

270 May it come soon
to the hungry
to the weeping
to those who thirst for your justice,
to those who have waited centuries
    for a truly human life.
Grant us the patience to smooth the way
    on which your Kingdom comes to us
Grant us hope, that we may not weary
    in proclaiming and working for it,
despite so many conflicts, threats and shortcomings.
Grant us a clear vision
    that in this hour of our history
    we may see the horizon
and know the way on which
    your Kingdom comes to us.

From a Nicaraguan meditation on the Lord's prayer

271 It's an amazing mystery!
Now, as never before – one world.
    From out of space, a ball of white and blue,
    yet alive with life – alive with people – one world,
    From its surface
    life and matter held in delicate balance – one world,
And humanity, with technical power to shape the world,
    and with decisive responsibility
    to use its resources in one world.
For the world is one.
    People can be fed and free;
    the homeless can have homes;
    the sick can have health;
    the hungry can be fed.
The vision is full of hope,
    Rejoice in it – accept it.
But there is a price to be paid,
    a dependence to be recognised,
Brothers and sisters to be acknowledged and loved.

Tony Jones, from *Prayers and Meditations*

Relationships...

272   **A song of Cain**

When man was in the jungle
Or, as some say, the garden,
He was not there alone
But one of many creatures
Small and great.
Our jungles now
Are made and lived in by ourselves.
And not much else survives
Except in cracks and crevices.
I find I miss my brothers.

W.S. Beattie

273   **Tomorrow's children**

Tomorrow's children cannot plead
nor the long-suffering earth protest
against today's destroyers;
nor can our forbears cry,
whose sacrifice and toil,
whose vision and whose faith
helped to create the fragile good
that we today enjoy,
the fragile good
that we so easily destroy
either by fear, or folly, or mistake.
Only through those who see and care today
the past, the future and the earth itself
can find a voice;
can plead for peace and life.
Dare we give them a voice to use?
Dare we refuse?

Basil Bridge

274 I saw you walking as I rounded the corner:
Your face as always
That perfectly conceived citadel
A master mason's pride
But grimly practical
Defending your heart.

I thought, dully, that you would ignore me:
But you turned half back
And stopped.

'Hullo', I cried and smiled at you,
Launching a weak attack against those towering walls
And shocked
Myself
And you
By tumbling through them.

Vivienne Stapley, *To L*

275 When my father died,
I never cried.
But when my geraniums looked wilted and sad,
I thought,
I'll phone and ask my dad,
And then I cried.

Denise Hopkins

276 She never told her love;
but let concealment,
like a worm in the bud,
feed on her damask cheek!

She sat, like Patience on a monument,
smiling at grief.

William Shakespeare, from *Twelfth Night*

277 Separation

Nothing can fill the gap when we are away
    from those we love, and it would be wrong
to try and find anything. We must simply
    hold out and win through. That sounds
very hard at first, but at the same time
    it is a great consolation, since leaving
the gap unfilled preserves the bonds between us.
    It is nonsense to say that God fills the gap;
he does not fill it, but keeps it empty
    so that our communion with another
may be kept alive, even at the cost of pain.

Dietrich Bonhoeffer

278 Health

By health I mean the power to live a full,
    adult, living, breathing life
in close contact with what I love –
    the earth and the wonders thereof –
the sea, the sun.
    All that we mean when we speak
of the eternal world.
    I want to enter into it,
to be part of it, to live in it,
    to learn from it, to lose all
that is superficial and acquired in me
    and to become a conscious direct
human being.
    I want, by understanding myself,
to understand others.
    I want to be all that I am capable
of becoming so that I may be
    a *child in the sun*.

Warm, eager, living life-
    to be rooted in life-
to learn, to desire to know,
    to feel, to think, to act.
That is what I want.

Katherine Mansfield

279 The Lord said,
'Say, "We" '
But I shook my head,
Hid my hands tight behind my back, and said,
Stubbornly,
'I.'

The Lord said,
'Say, "We" ';
But I looked upon them, grimy and all awry.
Myself in all those twisted shapes? Ah, no!
Distastefully I turned my head away,
Persisting,
'They.'

The Lord said,
'Say, "We" ';
And I
At last,
Richer by a hoard
Of years
And tears,
Looked in their eyes and formed the heavy word
That bent my neck and lowed my head:
Like a shamed schoolboy then I mumbled low,
'We,
Lord.'

Karle Wilson Baker

280 Lord,
when we pray for peace,
show us again and again,
that there can be no peace
without the establishment of justice,
and the renewal of integrity.

When we are tempted to retreat
into a sentimental peace of mind,
stir within us
the passion for justice which Amos had,
the social vision of Isaiah,
the international courage of Jeremiah,
and the personal responsibility of Hosea.

Then, Lord,
within the struggle,
for righteousness and equality,
for wholeness and honesty,
come to us with that special greeting
which you alone can provide,
dispelling our eternal fears,
cancelling our guilt,
refreshing our spirits:
the welcome, the peace, of your son,
Jesus Christ,
our Risen Lord.

David Jenkins

281   A wind of peace breathes
On the oceans of madness;
The night remains but the danger
Is gone.
Peace is here.
No pressure, no worries, no fears, no hopes,
Just silence and me.
Later the panic will come again;
Once more I will toss on the
Waves of blackness,
Once more I will wander on
Untrodden paths, again
I will cry and
No-one will answer,
But now, for this eternal second,
There is peace.

Catherine Baulch, 16 years

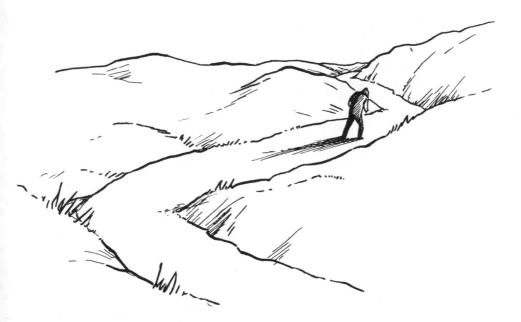

282 Peace was there.
     For a second it held out its arms
     And touched me.
     A light in the darkness
     Shone for a moment
     For me.
     But soon it wavered and died.
     Now, the lights are back
     On the edge of time;
     I am alone.
     Alone; now in a desert,
     Now on a hillside of darkness.
     There is no-one to help me,
     No shoulder to cry on.
     I am alone.
     I am me –
     That is life, and
     That is all of life.
     I must wander in silence for ever –
     Aimless drifting through
     Vast empty spaces
     Of echoing black –
     There is no way out of
     This maze.
     There is no escape.
     The whole of time stretches
     Into the distance.
     The whole of time.

     Catherine Baulch, 16 years

Creation...

283 **Rainbow's End?**

God gave us the radiant rainbow
The splendour and spectrum of love,
The message of Covenant mercy,
The olive-leaf borne by the dove.

We clutch in our terror and trembling
This delicate blue crystal ball;
Now high with the pride of possession;
Now desolate dread of its fall.

For we are the first generation
whose merciless scorning of love,
has the science to shatter all rainbows
the strength to destroy every dove.

The power to wither the olive
To cancel the promise of peace,
To order that Seedtime and Harvest
And Summer and Winter SHALL cease.

O Lord come again to your People
Forgive us and cleanse us we pray
that purged by the fire of your Spirit
We may waken to see your new day.

Come shatter our foolish delusions,
Cultivated within us from birth,
That we can be safe or be happy
At the cost of the rape of the Earth.

Come teach us afresh in this end-time,
The lore and the lesson of love
That to cling to our life is to lose it
To give and to trust, is to have.

Come show us afresh in our yearning,
The truth of your Cross and your strife,
That Easter is not for our earning,
That love is the lesson of life.

Kenyon E. Wright

284 The Great Chief in Washington sends word that he wishes to buy our land. The Great Chief also sends us words of friendship and good will. This is kind of him, since we know he has little need of friendship in return. But we will consider your offer, for we know if we do not do so, the white man may come with guns and take our land. What Chief Seathl says, the Great Chief in Washington can count on, as truly as our white brothers can count on the return of the seasons. My words are like the stars – they do not set.

How can you buy or sell the sky – the warmth of the land? The idea is strange to us. Yet we do not own the freshness of the air or the sparkle of the water. How can you buy them from us? We will decide in our time. Every part of this earth is sacred to my people. Every shining pine needle, every sandy shore, every mist in the dark woods, every clearing and humming insect is holy in the memory and experience of my people.

We know that the white man does not understand our ways. One portion of the land is the same to him as the next, for he is a stranger who comes in the night and takes from the land whatever he needs. The earth is not his brother, but his enemy, and when he has conquered it, he moves on. He leaves his fathers' graves behind and he does not care. He kidnaps the earth from his children. He does not care. His fathers' graves and his children's birthright are forgotten. His appetite will devour the earth and leave behind only a desert. The sight of your cities pains the eyes of the redman. But perhaps it is because the redman is savage and does not understand . . .

There is no quiet place in the white man's cities. No place to hear the leaves of spring or the rustle of insects' wings. But because perhaps I am a savage and do not understand, the clatter only seems to insult the ears. And what is there to life if a man cannot hear the lovely cry of the whippoorwill or the argument of the frogs around a pond at night? The Indian prefers the soft sound of the wind darting over the face of the pond, and the smell of the wind itself cleansed by a mid-day rain, or scented with pinion pine. The air is precious to the redman. For all things share the same breath – the beasts, the trees, the man. The white man does not seem to notice the air he breathes. Like a man dying for many days, he is numb to the smell of his own stench . . . When the last redman has vanished from the face of the earth, and the memory is only the shadow of a cloud moving across the prairie, these shores and forests will still hold the spirits of my people, for they love the earth as the newborn loves its mother's heartbeat.

If we sell you our land, love it as we've loved it. Care for it as we've cared for it. Hold in your mind the memory of the land, as it is when you take it.

And with all your strength, with all your might, and with all your heart preserve it for your children, and love it as God loves us all. One thing we know – our God is the same God. This earth is precious to him. Even the white man cannot be exempt from the common destiny.

Chief Seathl 1885

285   Father, it is one long catalogue of mistakes,
One good idea after another gone wrong;
Forgive us, and all whom we represent.
We farmed the land, and greedily took too much, ruining the soil.
We split the atom, and now it may destroy us,
We sailed the seas, and then fought the people we met
And still we go on.

We create parklands, and then can't create
   a society to appreciate them.
We build houses for shelter, and find them
   turning into over-populated cities.
We harvest the land, and then store the produce
   so that no one else can get it.

Father, forgive us, and teach us better ways.
Direct the creative powers you have given us
so that they turn to good not evil,
And though our foolishness must often make you weep
Still stay with us,
For Christ's sake.

                                 Amen.

Donald Hilton

286 **Hand it round first**

    . . .'I'm sure I don't know,' the Lion growled out as he lay down again.
'There was too much dust to see anything. What a time the Monster
is cutting up that cake!'
    Alice had seated herself on the bank of a little brook, with the great
dish on her knees, and was sawing away diligently with the knife.
'It's very provoking!' she said, in reply to the Lion (she was getting
quite used to being called 'the Monster'). I've cut several slices already,
but they always join on again!' 'You don't know how to manage
looking-glass cakes,' the Unicorn remarked. 'Hand it round first, and
cut it afterwards.'
    This sounded nonsense, but Alice very obediently got up, and
carried the dish round, and the cake divided itself into three pieces
as she did so. 'Now cut it up,' said the Lion, as she returned to her
place with the empty dish . . .

Lewis Carroll, from *Through the Looking Glass*

287   'Mummy, Oh Mummy, what's this pollution
That everyone's talking about?'
'Pollution's the mess that the country is in,
That we'd all be far better without.
It's factories belching their fumes in the air,
And the beaches all covered with tar,
Now throw all those sweet papers into the bushes
Before we get back in the car.'

'Mummy, Oh Mummy, who makes pollution,
And why don't they stop if it's bad?'
'Cos people like that just don't think about others,
They don't think at all, I might add.
They spray all the crops and they poison the flowers,
And wipe out the birds and the bees,
Now there's a good place we could dump that old mattress
Right out of sight in the trees.'

Mummy, Oh Mummy, what's going to happen
If all the pollution goes on?'
'Well the world will end up like a second-hand junk-yard,
With all of its treasures quite gone.
The fields will be littered with plastics and tins,
The streams will be covered with foam,
Now throw those two pop bottles over the hedge,
Save us from carting them home.'

'But Mummy, Oh Mummy, if I throw the bottles,
Won't that be polluting the wood?'
'Nonsense! that isn't the same thing at all,
You just shut up and be good.
If you're going to start getting silly ideas
I'm taking you home right away,
'Cos pollution is something that other folks do,
We're just enjoying our day.'

Anon

288   4,600 Million Years Old

If we condense this inconceivable time-span into an understandable concept, we can liken Earth to a person of 46 years of age.

Nothing is known about the first 7 years of this person's life, and whilst only scattered information exists about the middle span, we know that only at the age of 42 did the Earth begin to flower.

Dinosaurs and the great reptiles did not appear until one year ago, when the planet was 45. Mammals arrived only 8 months ago; in the middle of last week man-like apes evolved into ape-like men, and at the weekend the last ice age enveloped the Earth. Modern man has been around for 4 hours. During the last hour man discovered agriculture. The industrial revolution began a minute ago.

During those sixty seconds of biological time, modern man has made a rubbish tip of Paradise.

He has multiplied his numbers to plague proportions, caused the extinction of 500 species of animals, ransacked the planet for fuels and now stands like a brutish infant, gloating over this meteoric rise to ascendancy, on the brink of a war to end all wars and of effectively destroying this oasis of life in the solar system.

Greenpeace

289   To us the land is a living thing
The land is our mother.
It is the source of our existence,
our religion, our identity.
To us land is a living thing.
We are part of it
and it is part of us.

An Australian Aborigine

290   Enjoy the earth gently
Enjoy the earth gently
For if the earth is spoiled
It cannot be repaired
Enjoy the earth gently.

Yoruba Poem, West Africa

291   Planet Earth

God was sitting in His garden, in the evening, with His gin
(For the joys of creativity were wearing rather thin)
He had drafted out the Universe, and calculated π
Then He saw a barren, blue-green ball suspended in the sky.
'I'll create a whole new planet with high mountains and deep seas
And a billion different life-forms from great dinosaurs to trees,
And the balance will be perfect, Nature's harmony complete –
Until I create a primate that walks upright, on two feet.
These said creatures shall be jealous – they'll make wars and
    want to fight,
They will have a sense of logic, so they can't tell wrong from right.
Out of all the different life-forms there, they'll be the most confused,
With their things they call 'society' and even 'moral views'.
I shall colour them in every hue, from black to milky white,
They'll play games of 'race relations' and of 'basic human rights',
And so that they haven't got a hope of knowing what to do,
I shall make them eleven sexes but say there are only two.
I will give them 'state economies' and drugs to dull their minds,
So that they think they know about the safety of mankind,
While their world expires around them, and the sands
    of time run dry,
While the piles of deadly weapons rear against the clear blue sky.'
Then God broke off, for the thought somehow did not appeal to Him
Of a planet's own destruction – so He polished off His gin,
But the thought was not forgotten, for, before the sun had set,
God had catalogued Earth's blueprint in His filing cabinet.
And, there, on His coloured memo pad (with ball-point, done in red)
The clear headline 'Eve and Adam' could quite obviously be read.

Sarah Sarkhel, 16 years

292 A Bright Future?

Twinkle, Twinkle, little Earth,
How I wonder what you're worth.
Chopping forests by the score,
Soon we won't have any more.

Twinkle, Twinkle, planet fair,
What is happening in your air?
Acid rain and airborne lead,
Pretty soon we'll all be dead.

Twinkle, Twinkle, on the sea,
Floating oil and foul debris.
Sewage floating by the shore,
Killing bathers by the score.

Twinkle, Twinkle, planet blue,
Animals are going too,
Chemicals and pesticides,
Causing deaths and suicides.

Twinkle, Twinkle, disco star,
Getting noisier by the bar,
Concorde's roar and jumbo jet,
And it's getting noisier yet!

Twinkle, Twinkle, earthly light,
Glowing brightly in the night.
Caesium, plutonium,
Radon and uranium.

Twinkle, Twinkle, in the sky,
Watch the cruising missiles fly.
Fire a laser, drop a bomb,
Now all the pollution's gone!

Andrew Dawson, 12 years

293 The Rock Pool

I was walking along the beach
When I saw a pool.
The waves were plastic bottles
And the pebbles were bottle tops.
The ripples were silver paper
And toffee wrappers swam around like fish.

Then I remembered a pool
Where the pebbles were solid gold
And the ripples were
Silver stars
And rainbow fish darted
Through crystal water.

Alex Marples, 8 years

294   And I, the Earth the Lord created
Cry aloud to my Maker,
Save me from ravage and destruction
To praise and glorify your name forever.

Mountains and hills, plants and trees,
Rivers and oceans, whales and fishes,
Birds, beasts and cattle,
Cry aloud to the Lord,
Save us from destruction
To praise and magnify you forever.

Save us! Save us! Save us!

O all we children of the Lord,
Cry aloud to the Lord,
We are those who destroy.
Save us to be your people
To praise and glorify your name forever.

Save us! Save us! Save us!

Martin Palmer

295   God bless the field and bless the furrow,
Stream and branch and rabbit burrow,
Hill and stone and flower and tree,
From Bristol town to Wetherby –
Bless the sun and bless the sleet.
Bless the lane and bless the street,
Bless the night and bless the day,
Bless all travellers on their way
Bless the minnow, bless the whale,
Bless the rainbow and the hail,
Bless the nest and bless the leaf,
Bless the righteous and the thief,
Bless the wing and bless the fin,
Bless the air I travel in,
Bless the mill and bless the mouse,
Bless the family in their house,
Bless the earth and bless the sea,
God bless you and God bless me.

Anon

296   A Lesson

The End of the World will be filmed
Thirty times over.
And given the 'Comment' part on Channel 4.
The End of the World will be
A theme tune
A book
A film
A T-shirt
And an hour-part drama serial
Covered on 'Did You See?'

The End of the World will be a poster
On every slab of rubble
To remind us all of the power
We possessed,
The power we abused.

The End of the World will be reviewed
By a best-selling author
And shown on 'Bookmark'.

The End of the World will be broadcast
Throughout a nation
That's been dead
For thirty years.

The End of the World will be a lesson
To us all.
But none of us will learn.

Sinead Morrissey, 14 years

297 Contra-genesis

On the last day man destroyed the world called Earth.
Earth had been beautiful
until the spirit of man moved across her face
destroying all things.

And man said, 'Let there be darkness.'
Man found the darkness to be good
and called it 'Security'.
And man divided himself
into races and religions and social classes.
And there was neither dusk nor dawn
on the seventh day before all ended.

And man said, 'Let there be a strong government
to reign over our darkness.
Let there be armies so we can kill each other
with order and efficiency in the darkness;
Let us hunt and destroy those who tell the truth,
here and unto the ends of the earth,
for we like our darkness.'
And there was neither dusk nor dawn
on the sixth day before all ended.

And man said, 'Let there be rockets and bombs
so we can kill more quickly and easily.'
And there were gas chambers and ovens
to better finish the task.
It was the fifth day before all ended.

And man said, 'Let there be drugs
and other means of escape;
for there is this slight but constant irritant
- called REALITY –
that disturbs our comfort.'
It was the fourth day before all ended.

And man said, 'Let there be divisions between the nations
so we can know
the name of our enemy.'
It was the third day before all ended.

Finally man said,
'Let us make God in our image and likeness,
so no other God will arise to compete with us.
Let us say that God thinks as we think,
hates as we hate,
and kills as we kill.'
It was the second day before all ended.

On the last day
a great blast shook the face of the Earth;
Fire purged that beautiful terrestial ball,
and all was silent.

And the Lord God saw
What man had done,
And in the silence
that engulfed the smoking ruins,
God wept.

Anonymous, Nicaragua

ACKNOWLEDGEMENTS

The compiler and publishers express thanks for permission to use copyright items. Every effort has been made to trace copyright owners but if any rights have been inadvertently overlooked, the necessary correction will gladly be made in subsequent editions.

Copyright permissions are listed in item order. Where more than one item derives from the same copyright source item numbers for later entries are indicated in brackets after the first entry.

Item

1   (176, 249) From *Markings* by Dag Hammarskjöld translated by W.H. Auden and Leif Sjoberg. Reprinted by permission of Faber & Faber Ltd

3   From *Mere Christianity* by C.S. Lewis. Reprinted by permission of Collins Ltd

4   (42, 67, 77, 180, 272) Reprinted by permission of author

6   (291-293, 296) From *The Earthsick Astronaut*. Reprinted by permission of The Observer National Children's Poetry Competition and several authors

8   (9, 92) From *The Tower of Babel* by Morris West. Reprinted by permission of William Heinemann Ltd

10   From *Noah* by Andre Obey, translated by Arthur Wilmert. Reprinted by permission of William Heinemann Ltd

12   (13, 14, 86, 87, 89, 104) Frm *What It's Like To Be Me* compiled by Richard Exley. Reprinted by permission of compiler

16   Reprinted by permission of author

17   Reprinted by permission of The Very Revd John F. Petty, Provost of Coventry

18   Reprinted by permission of author

19   (121) Reprinted by permission of author

20   (105, 179, 211, 234) Reprinted by permission of The World Council of Churches, Geneva, Switzerland

21   (55) From *The Rabbit Skin Cap* by George Baldry. Reprinted by permission of Cmdr. M.E. Cheyne

23   (182) From *Some Day I'll Find You* by H.R. Williams. Reprinted by permission of Mitchell Beazley

29   Reprinted by permission of author

30   Source unknown. Reprinted by permission of Collins

31   Reprinted by permission of author

32   (37, 188) Reprinted by permission of author

39   From *Amadeus* by Peter Shaffer. Reprinted by permission of Andre Deutsch

40   From *Bruno's Dream* by Iris Murdoch. Reprinted by permission of Chatto & Windus

41   (79) Reprinted by permission of Macmillan, London and Basingstoke

43   First printed in *Moments of Truth* (1990) published by Marshall Pickering. Reprinted by permission of author who retains copyright

45   From *Assembled in Britain* published by Marshall Pickering. Reprinted by permission of author

46   Reprinted by permission of author

47   Reprinted by permission of author

50   From *Teilhard De Chardin* by Vernon Sproxton. Reprinted by permission of SCM Press

52   From *Straw Hats and Serge Bloomers* by Eileen Elias. Published 1979. Reprinted by permission of W.H. Allen & Co

53   (66) Reprinted by permission of author

59   From *Testimonies of Faith*. Reprinted by permission of World Alliance of Reformed Churches, Geneva

61   (90, 111, 246, 250) Reprinted by permission of author

63   From *The Place Where Socks Go* by Godfrey Rust. Reprinted by permission of Asset Publications

64   Reprinted by permission of author

73   From *Selly Oak Colleges Occasional Paper 2*. Reprinted by permission of the President, Martin Conway

75   (177) Reprinted by permission of The Alister Hardy Research Centre

88   (97, 98, 100, 164, 198, 229, 260) From *No Longer Strangers* edited by Iben Gjerding and Katherine Kinnamon. Reprinted by permission of The Lutheran World Federation

91   From *The Observer*, December 20 1988. Reprinted with permission

93   From *The Mysticism of Paul The Apostle* by Albert Schweitzer. Reprinted by permission of Grafton Books, a division of HarperCollins

94   From *USPG Network* (April 1984). Reprinted by permission of The United Society for the Propogation of the Gospel

95   Reprinted by permission of WWF/ICOREC

96   Reprinted by permission of author and Calcutta Urban Service

99   (118) Reprinted by permission of Mr. Alfred Willetts

106 From *A Statement of Commitment by Christian Aid Board July 1987*. Reprinted by permission of Christian Aid

108 (110, 117, 123, 138, 193, 204, 205) From *The Violence of Love*, The Words of Oscar Romero (1988). Reprinted by permission of Collins

113 Reprinted by permission of SOS Childrens Villages UK

114 From *The Collected Poems of A.S.J. Tessimond* with translations from Jacques Prevert, edited by Hubert Nicholson, Whiteknights Press, 1985. Reprinted with permission

116 Reprinted by permission of author

120 From *Compassionate and Free* by Marianne Katoppo. Permission sought from the Christian Conference of Asia

124 (149, 159, 169) Reprinted by permission of author

125 (136) From *Children of Asia and Suffering and Hope* Reprinted by permission of The Christian Conference of Asia

126 Reprinted by permission of author

127 Source unknown. Reprinted by permission of Collins

128 (129, 137, 197) Reprinted by permission of author

132 Reprinted by permission of author

133 (141, 165) Reprinted by permission of author

139 From *A Giant's Scrapbook* by Stewart Henderson published by Hodder & Stoughton. Reprinted by permission of author

140 Reprinted by permission of Church News Service

143 From *The Shadow of the Galilean* by Gerd Theissen. Reprinted by permission of SCM Press

147 Reprinted by permission of author

151 From *The Shape of the Liturgy* by Dom Gregory Dix. Reprinted by permission of A & C Black

154 Reprinted by permission of *The New Internationalist*

162 Reprinted by permission of World Alliance of Reformed Churches, Geneva

163 Reprinted by permission of author

166 (280) Reprinted by permission of author

167 Reprinted by permission of *The Listener*

168 From *Telephone Poles* by John Updike. Reprinted by permission of Andre Deutsch

172 Reprinted by permission of Mrs. Mary G. Lewis

174 From *Living Poems – Making Eden Grow*. Reprinted by permission of author

181 Reprinted by permission of author

187 *What Is Truth?* by Ted Hughes. Reprinted by permission of Faber & Faber

189 From *The Right to Believe* 1989; 3. Reprinted by permission of Keston College

191 (192, 208, 209, 223, 231, 242) Reprinted from *Now* where the items were used with permission

199 Reprinted by permission of The British Broadcasting Corporation

200 From *Christian Aid Christmas Leaflet* 1989. Reprinted by permission of Christian Aid

202 From *The World Calls Christians to Prayer*. Reprinted by permission of The Methodist Church Overseas Division

206 From *Grey is the Colour of Hope* by Irina Ratushinskaya. Reprinted by permission of Hodder & Stoughton Ltd

215 Reprinted by permission of author

216 From *Without a City Wall* by Melvyn Bragg. Reprinted by permission of Hodder & Stoughton

217 Reprinted by permission of author

221 Quoted in *Candles in the Dark* by Mary Craig. Reprinted by permission of Hodder & Stoughton

224 First printed in *The Moravian Messenger*. Reprinted by permission of author

226 First printed in the *Herald* August 1985. Reprinted by permission of The Baptist Missionary Society

227 From *Assembled in Britain* by Stewart Henderson published by Hodder & Stoughton. Reprinted by permission of author

228 Reprinted by permission of author

230 From *Information Service* 1983/I-II. Reprinted by permission of Pontificium Consilium Ad Christianorum Unitatem Fovendam

232 From *Candles in the Dark* by Mary Craig. Reprinted by permission of Hodder & Stoughton

236 Reprinted by permission of author

237 Reprinted by permission of author

238 From *Love's Endeavour, Love's Response* by W.H. Vanstone, published and copyright 1977 by Darton, Longman and Todd Ltd. Used by permission of the publishers

243 (262) Reprinted by permission of Stainer & Bell Ltd

244 From Justice, Peace and the Integrity of Creation material produced for the Seoul Conference 1990. Reprinted by permission of the World Council of Churches, Geneva, Switzerland.

247 From *The Go-Between God* by John V. Taylor. Reprinted by permission of S.C.M. Press

251 Reprinted by permission of author
252 Reprinted by permission of The Hogarth Press Ltd
253 Reprinted by permission of author
258 From *Walking on Thorns* by Alan Boesak. Reprinted by permission of the World Council of Churches. Geneva, Switzerland
261 Reprinted by permission of the Lutheran World Federation
267 Published by the Latin American Conference of Churches. This translation first appeared in *Now*. Used with permission
269 From *Faith Looking Forward*. Reprinted by permission of Oxford University Press
271 From *Prayers and Meditations* by Tony Jones. Reprinted by permission of Christian Aid
273 Reprinted by permission of author
281 (282) Reprinted by permission of author
288 Reprinted by permission of Greenpeace
292 Reprinted by permission of author
294 From *Creation Festival Liturgy*. Reprinted by permission of WWF/ICOREC

INDEX OF AUTHORS

Where the author is not known, the source is given

INDEX OF SUBJECTS

INDEX OF FIRST LINES